Does Class Matter
Social Stratification and Orientations in Singapore

Tan Ern Ser
National University of Singapore

Does Class Matter

Social Stratification and Orientations in Singapore

World Scientific

NEW JERSEY · LONDON · SINGAPORE · BEIJING · SHANGHAI · HONG KONG · TAIPEI · CHENNAI

Published by

World Scientific Publishing Co. Pte. Ltd.
5 Toh Tuck Link, Singapore 596224
USA office: Suite 202, 1060 Main Street, River Edge, NJ 07661
UK office: 57 Shelton Street, Covent Garden, London WC2H 9HE

British Library Cataloguing-in-Publication Data
A catalogue record for this book is available from the British Library.

DOES CLASS MATTER?
Social Stratification and Orientations in Singapore

Copyright © 2004 by World Scientific Publishing Co. Pte. Ltd.

All rights reserved. This book, or parts thereof, may not be reproduced in any form or by any means, electronic or mechanical, including photocopying, recording or any information storage and retrieval system now known or to be invented, without written permission from the Publisher.

For photocopying of material in this volume, please pay a copying fee through the Copyright Clearance Center, Inc., 222 Rosewood Drive, Danvers, MA 01923, USA. In this case permission to photocopy is not required from the publisher.

ISBN 981-238-829-X

Typeset by Stallion Press

Printed in Singapore.

Dedicated to

my wife Bee

and

our sons Caleb and Cephas

Contents

Acknowledgements		ix
1	Singapore: Market Economy and Meritocratic, Middle-Class Society?	1
2	Methodology: Questionnaire, Sampling, and Fieldwork	7
3	Singapore Class Structure	9
4	Social Orientations by Class, Age, and Ethnicity	20
5	Work Career and Social Mobility	47
6	Problem Areas: Digital Divide and Sandwich Generation	59
7	1-to-2 Roomers, 3-Roomers, and Citizen Population Compared	66
8	Conclusion: Does Class Matter in Singapore?	83
Appendix I Six Case Studies		87
Appendix II Opinion Research Questionnaire		110
Bibliography		127
Index		129

Acknowledgements

It is not possible for anyone to run a survey alone, without involving many other people and organizations.

I am therefore most grateful for the assistance I received from the Ministry of Community Development and Sports, and particularly from the Strategic Policy and Research Division.

I am also appreciative of the cooperation I received from the many respondents to the survey. They have so willingly given of their time to answer a fairly long questionnaire. Without their inputs, there will be no tables and case studies to report.

However, I must add that, although this book has benefited from the people acknowledged above, I alone am responsible for its contents.

Tan Ern Ser
January 2004

1

Singapore: Market Economy and Meritocratic, Middle-Class Society?

Introduction

Class or stratification is a fundamental dimension of social life. It is, as Bottomore (1965:14) points out, "deeply involved in many of the most vital questions of modern politics and social policy". A good grasp of the character of social stratification in a society can therefore facilitate our understanding of the key social and political issues confronting that society as well as the social orientations of people located within it.

This book, which is based on a 2001 study on social stratification in Singapore, has three main objectives: (a) to map out the class structure in Singapore; (b) to examine the relationship between class position and social orientations towards opportunity, welfarism, political participation, class and ethnic relations, trade unionism, and Singapore understood as a nation and economy; and (c) to identify problem areas (e.g. digital divide, sandwich generation), and economic and social consequences (e.g. social mobility) associated with class position.

The findings reported in this book are derived from a national survey covering 2250 Singaporeans aged 15–64 years. To compare the general population with "lower income" Singaporeans, the survey also interviewed a smaller sample of 500 respondents living in one-, two-, or three-room Housing and Development Board (HDB) flats (see findings in Chapter 7). The survey fieldwork was conducted during the period from March to April and from June to July 2001.

The analyses involved in this study entail, as a starting point, a good theoretical framework by which to understand Singapore society. The key concepts and theoretical issues will be dealt with in the rest of this chapter.

Middle-class society, not equal to classless society

Singapore is a meritocratic society that operates on the basis of equality of opportunity and rewarding by performance. Logically, this does not make it a classless society, since equal opportunity does not necessarily lead to equal outcomes, and rewarding by merit assumes unequal attainments. Indeed, Singapore society is characterized by a hierarchy of positions with unequal power, authority, resources, and rewards. Moreover, as a capitalist society, rewards are, to a large extent, determined by market forces, which favour some kinds of skills or credentials over others at different points in time. At the same time, people are not equally endowed in terms of motivation, ability, aptitude, and material and cultural capital. Hence, despite the policy of equalization of opportunities, the life-chances and lifestyles of different segments of the population are unlikely to be equal, though the extent of inequality could be reduced.

What a market economy can logically strive to achieve is to create a middle-class society—not a classless society—where all citizens have access to education, housing, and healthcare, and where those who have acquired the necessary skills and qualifications are able to secure employment and decent wages. To qualify as a middle-class society, a large majority of the citizenry must meet the criteria of having a secondary or higher education, home ownership, and urban consumption (Yao, 1996:339).

Can Singapore be considered a middle-class society then? Back in the mid-1970s, Chen (1975:22) was already arguing that, gauging from income and social mobility data, Singapore was a middle-class society. In the late 1980s, the label came into prominence when the then Prime Minister Lee Kuan Yew said that "Singapore is a middle class society" based primarily on the criterion that more than 80 per cent of Singaporeans owned the property they lived in (*Straits Times*, 14 August 1987). More recently, Mak (1993:309) suggested that "the size of the middle class (in Singapore) has been growing since the 1970s, surpassing the working class in size."

Middle-class society, not equal to one-class society

However, it is not a straightforward exercise to arrive at a consensus on whether or not a "middle-class society" has indeed been achieved in Singapore. Rodan (1993:54), for instance, cited Quah *et al.*'s (1991:262) observation that there was "no evidence of a concentration of people in one homogenous 'middle' interval", while Chua and Tan (1999:154) argued that "the relative homogenization of daily life, as a result of extensive and standardized provision of collective consumption goods to the overwhelming majority of the population, has glossed over class differences, giving the impression that Singapore is 'homogeneously' a middle-class society." The apparent homogeneity could also be due to "the fact that the distinctive middle class aspirations are shared by those lower on the socio-economic ladder" (Yao, 1996:339). Another angle on the homogeneity thesis is reflected in Deputy Prime Minister Lee Hsien Loong's observation that "the clear divide between workers and employers is breaking down, as more workers receive share options and become stakeholders in the companies they work for" (*Straits Times*, 30 September 1999).

On balance, if one takes into consideration the low unemployment rate, the high literacy rate, and the high rates of upward social mobility over the last three decades, there is a case for arguing that Singapore is a middle-class society, which does not mean that it is a one-class society, but that it has a large majority with life-chances and lifestyles normally associated with the middle class, and only a small proportion of low income people.

There have been various estimates of the proportion of poor people in Singapore. A recent *Straits Times* report (3 December 2001) puts the figure as 120 000 individuals or 4 per cent of the resident population of 3 million people. Census 2000 data indicate that about 8 per cent of Singaporeans live in households with a total monthly income of below $1000, about 3 per cent of citizens live in one- or two-room HDB flats, and 22 per cent in three-room HDB flats. These figures in themselves may overestimate the extent of poverty, as a person with low household income—below $1000—or living in a small public flat may have accumulated some savings from past employment or investment.[1] What is certain, however, is that towards the higher end of the social ladder, Singapore can boast of 72 per cent of its citizens living in HDB four-room apartments or higher priced housing units; 57 per cent of working citizens in non-manual occupations; and 40 per cent of working citizens attaining at least upper secondary educational qualifications (Census, 2000).

The new middle-class society

The above positive profile has by now been very much identified with Singapore. After all, Singapore is known as one of the successful East Asian tigers, though this label has lost some of its glitter following the 1997 Asian economic crisis. With the current economic downturn, which surfaced in early 2001 and deepening after the September 11 incident in the United States that year, there are indications that the job and income security and aspirations normally associated with the middle class and hopeful working class may no longer be realistic. A recent *Business Times* (14 December 2001) report observed that "four in 10 of the 9000 people retrenched in the first half of this year (2001) were executives." Another news report (*Straits Times*, 15 December 2001) revealed that 16 500 tertiary educated Singaporeans were jobless in September 2001.

Perhaps, instead of the upward mobility and "upgrading" mentality that characterized Singapore in the last two decades, the current recession, together with the restructuring of the economy, may

---

[1] The implication here is that, to determine class position, it is often necessary to gather information on wealth, apart from income, housing, education, and occupation.

produce a different kind of middle-class Singaporeans: one more accustomed to not only belt-tightening, job and income insecurity, downgrading, and downward mobility, but also to employment flexibility, lifelong skills upgrading, risk-taking, and entrepreneurship. If this turns out to be the case, the middle-class society in Singapore at the turn of the century would be qualitatively different from that of the 1980s and 1990s, even if both were given the same label.

Thus far, we have attempted to clarify that conceptually Singapore can be understood as a middle-class society, even though it has a fairly large working class as well as a small proportion of poor people. We have also argued that Singapore, the middle-class society at the turn of the new millennium, may be qualitatively different from that of Singapore, the middle-class society and East Asian tiger of the 1980s and 1990s. Given that the bulk of the fieldwork for this study was conducted in the early half of 2001, the survey data would enable us to throw some light on Singapore's class structure and related social orientations at the turn of the twenty-first century and amidst an economic condition best described as the "new insecurity" brought about by globalization (Byrne, 1999).

Class or stratification?

Before we move on to examine the survey data on class structure and social orientations in Singapore, we will deal with one more important conceptual issue, which is to consider whether Singapore should be understood as a class society or as a stratified society. A class society, by Marxian definition, is characterized by class conflict, tension, and struggle, and, possibly, eventual transformation into a socialist society; while a stratified society suggests unequal life-chances, a Weberian definition, but no inherent class conflict and potential transformation into a classless society.

Ideologically, the class perspective does not sit comfortably with the nation-building project superimposed upon a capitalist economy, as the class inequality and conflict associated with capitalism must somehow be reconciled with the idea of citizenship; and national identity, solidarity, and unity—captured by the slogan "one people, one nation". In contrast, within the stratification perspective, social inequality can be rendered compatible with nation-building via a system of equality of opportunity and meritocracy for all citizens, tempered by state welfarism and community charity for the needy.

For the purpose of this study, I would argue that a theoretically sound approach is to adopt the Weberian perspective, which is to think of class in terms of life-chances, which may or may not be a source of social tension, conflict, or change in a predetermined direction. Such an approach resonates with that of Marshall (1997:50–52). In a non-trivial sense, using this approach also means that the different categories or levels of life-chances could be conveniently labelled as classes, and the broad topic of this study as social stratification.

The next chapter outlines the methodology and methods used in the survey that provide the data for this book.

2

Methodology: Questionnaire, Sampling, and Fieldwork

Questionnaire

The survey instrument used in this study is an eight-page questionnaire (see Appendix II). Its design benefited from 32 in-depth interview case materials gathered prior to the survey. Six of these cases are presented in Appendix I.

The final questionnaire was translated into Chinese, Malay, and Tamil from English. The questionnaire is divided into six sections. Section A comprises the screening questions and some demographic variables. Section B focuses on job history and training. Section C asks about financial situation, including utilization of the services of social agencies or programmes. Section D deals with social orientations towards political participation, opportunity, welfarism, social justice, class and ethnic relations, unionism, financial support for dependents, and Singapore understood as an economy and nation. Section E looks at the subjective class identification of respondents, while Section F solicits other demographic information not covered in Section A. It takes about 20–30 minutes to administer the questionnaire in each face-to-face interview.

Two samples

Face-to-face interviews were conducted on a national representative sample covering the entire island. The sample size is 2250. It is a disproportionate, random sample of Singapore citizens aged 15–64 years, stratified by ethnicity, comprising 965 Chinese (43 per cent), 645 Malays (29 per cent), 515 Indians (23 per cent), and 125 "Others" (6 per cent). This means that the majority Chinese were under-sampled, while the minorities were over-sampled. The rationale for this sampling approach was to ensure that there would be sufficient cases of minority Singaporeans for statistical analysis. However, the results reported in this study are based on the weighted sample, which reflects the actual ethnic composition of the citizen population. The study also involves a "lower income" sample comprising 500 respondents living in one-, two-, or three-room HDB flats.

Fieldwork

The fieldwork was conducted during March–April and June–July 2001. Despite the voluntary character of the survey, the data collection phase managed to achieve a credible response rate of about 80 per cent.

Several factors contributed to this healthy response rate. A letter soliciting the cooperation of potential respondents was mailed out to those listed in the randomly generated sample. Prior to the survey proper, the questionnaire was put through a pilot test in January–February 2001. The questionnaire was subsequently modified on the basis of the feedback from the pilot phase. The final version of the questionnaire is relatively short, contains mostly close-ended items and, therefore, very user-friendly. Proper training and close supervision of interviewers were emphasized throughout the fieldwork phase.

The next five chapters (Chapters 3–7) will report and discuss the survey findings.

3

Singapore Class Structure

Classificatory schemes

Most early studies on social stratification conceptualized a rather straightforward class structure consisting of two broad classes: manual and non-manual; white-collar and blue-collar; or middle-class and working-class. This simplified model of class structure continues to be widely used, as it provides a parsimonious device to capture an otherwise complex phenomenon and process.

At about the same time, in the 1950s, some researchers introduced sub-categories like skilled, semi-skilled, and unskilled blue-collar workers. Similarly, the white-collar segment was sub-divided into professionals, managers, and routine white-collar workers. This classification is not entirely new, it being the template used by US census-takers even in the early 1940s, such as Alba Edwards (see Barber, 1957).

More recently, in the 1980s and 1990s, the literature narrowed down to two theoretically informed classificatory systems: the Wright and Goldthorpe systems. Wright adopts a Marxian perspective, while Goldthorpe uses the Weberian approach (Edgell, 1993). Wright's class map has 12 class locations defined by three dimensions: ownership or non-ownership of capital, ownership or non-ownership of skills or credentials, and ownership or non-ownership of organizational authority. Goldthorpe's class scheme has primarily seven categories classified in terms of possession of job security, career advancement, and work authority and autonomy or, more generally, work and market situations (Edgell, 1993:27). These categories can in turn be grouped into three broad classes: service class, intermediate class, and working class.

For the purpose of this study, whenever occupational status is used as an indicator of class, I shall utilize Goldthorpe's class scheme, rather than Wright's class map, as its "unidimensionality", like the simple two-class model, provides a simple yet fruitful approach for handling the complex data and understanding the impact of class position on social orientations and mobility. But unidimensionality does have its own conceptual problems, in particular that relating to the rank ordering of classes.

To overcome such limitations, as well as complement Goldthorpe's class scheme, I will utilize cluster analysis to develop a multidimensional class map of Singapore. The clusters will be based on total monthly personal income and education and cross-tabulated with occupation. Unfortunately, this approach is meaningful only when applied to those who are in paid employment, which excludes housewives, students, and retirees. Hence, there is a need for a classification which can cover the entire sample, and thereby the Singapore population.

After some "experimentations" with the dataset, including scrutinizing numerous cluster analysis outputs, I found a viable alternative in the subjective four-category class map. The latter can serve as an effective, convenient indicator of a comprehensive Singapore class structure (see later sections in this chapter for more details on the four-category class map).

Where available, comparative figures from Census 2000 would be placed alongside the relevant survey data. These also serve as a check on the extent to which the survey data deviate from the corresponding census data. However, it should be noted that while the survey was conducted in 2001, the census was carried out in 2000. Given that the economy has experienced the onset of recession in

2001, our survey data therefore provide a first glimpse of the impact of the current recession on class structure and social orientations in Singapore.

Is Singapore a middle-class society?

This section will present both the objective indicators (occupation, income, education) as well as the subjective indicators (self-identification) of class in Singapore.

Table 3.1 shows the occupational status of Singaporeans aged 15–64 years who are currently working. Both Census 2000 and Survey 2001 indicate that between two-thirds and three-fourths of working Singaporeans could be classified as middle-class, defined as the proportion of those in the service and intermediate classes.

Somewhat similar, Table 3.2, which presents the results of a SPSS-generated cluster analysis[2] based on total monthly personal income and education of working Singaporeans, indicates that 76 per cent are in the intermediate and service classes. In terms of monthly household income, and using the median income of $3607 as the dividing line between working class and middle class, Census 2000 suggests that 63 per cent of citizen households could be classified as middle-class or higher, while Survey 2001 has a lower figure of 48 per cent (see Table 3.3).

Table 3.1 Occupational status of working citizens (per cent)

Occupational status	Survey 2001	Census 2000
Service class: managers, professionals, associate professionals	48) 74	41) 69
Intermediate class: clerical, service workers	26)	28)
Working class: skilled, semi-skilled, unskilled workers	26	31
Total ($N = 1456$)	100	100

---

[2] The clusters were generated using the Analyse-Classify-*K*-Means Cluster procedure in SPSS. After which, they were cross-tabulated against the variable "Goldthorpe class categories". The latter variable was itself a derivative of the variable "current occupation". The cluster with a majority of cases in Goldthorpe's service class was, accordingly, labelled as "Service Class". The same procedure was used to identify the "Intermediate Class" and "Working Class" clusters.

Table 3.2 Class cluster of working citizens (per cent)

Cluster	Per cent
Service class	33) 76
Intermediate class	43)
Working class	20
Others	4
Total ($N=1456$)	100

Table 3.3 Total monthly income of citizen households (per cent)

Income category	Survey 2001	Census 2000
$8000 and over	7) 48	18) 63
$3000–7999	41)	45)
$1000–2999	40	28
Below $1000	8	8
Refused/DK	4	NA
Total ($N=2248$)	100	100

Tables 3.4 (on educational attainment) and 3.5 (on housing type) reinforce the view that between two-thirds and three-fourths of citizens are in the middle class. Both of these dimensions reflect the outcomes of the PAP Government's welfare policy and provisions. According to Mak (1993:332), the "Singapore government has been the principal architect in creating (the middle class)". Similarly, Rodan (1996:37) argued that the middle class is the "major beneficiary of PAP rule". However, while the numbers on these two dimensions cut a beautiful profile, they may, in a recession, mask a less than comfortable picture, insofar as educational attainment may not always be translated into employment, job security, or career advancement, and the housing type that symbolizes middle-classness may sometimes turn out to be more of a liability than an asset, should there be a drop in property prices or a loss of ability to service housing loans.

The data reported above pertain to several objective indicators of class. We shall now consider three subjective indicators of class.

Singapore Class Structure 13

Table 3.4 Educational attainment of citizens (per cent)

Educational attainment	Survey 2001	Census 2000
University	10) 76	10) 67
Diploma	11)	11)
Upper secondary	11)	10)
Secondary	44)	36)
Primary	20	13
No qualification	4	21
Total ($N = 2248$)	100	100

Table 3.5 Housing type of citizens (per cent)

Housing type	Survey 2001	Census 2000
Landed property	5) 73	6) 75
Private apartment	3)	6)
HDB Five-room and executive	26)	27)
Four-room	39)	36)
Three-room	24	22
One-and two-room	3	3
Total ($N = 2248$)	100	100

Table 3.6, focusing on perceived current financial situation, indicates that 90 per cent of Singapore citizens considered themselves to be "average" or "above average". If being "average" is a rough gauge for in at least the lower middle class, then it may be argued that a vast majority of Singaporeans are middle class. However, this is a rather blunt instrument for capturing subjective class. Hence, following other stratification studies, Survey 2001 also asked respondents to place themselves on a six-category class ladder and on a four-category class ladder.

The subjective class structure shows a pattern which resembles those of earlier studies (see Zweig, 2000:57–58). When asked to place themselves in the six-category class ladder comprising upper class, three middle-class categories, and two lower-class categories, an overwhelming 87 per cent of the respondents identified themselves as middle class (Table 3.7). This finding is quite similar to that of the equivalent 1983 data reported in Quah *et al.* (1991).

Table 3.6 Perceived financial situation as an indicator of class structure

Perceived present financial situation	Per cent
Well-off	1) 90
Better than average	16)
Average	73)
Poor	10
Total ($N=2250$)	100

Table 3.7 Class structure (subjective): Six-category and four-category class ladders compared

Six-category class ladder	Quah, et al. 1991	Survey 2001	Survey 2001	Four-category class ladder
Upper class	1	1	2	Upper class
Upper middle class	5) 82	6) 87		
Middle middle class	44)	49)	42	Middle class
Lower middle class	33)	32)		
Upper lower class	12) 17	9) 12	51	Working class
Lower lower class	5)	3)	6	Lower class
Total ($N=2250$)	100	100	100	

Comparing the two time points, there seems to be a 5 per cent perceived upward mobility from the lower class to the middle class.

What is perhaps more interesting is that when the respondents were asked to place themselves in the four-category class ladder (upper class, middle class, working class, and lower class), about half of the self-identified middle-class respondents and half of the self-identified lower-class in the six-category class ladder immediately changed their classification to working class. Hence, in terms of the latter subjective indicator of class, the class structure that emerged suggests that Singapore may be characterized as a mix of middle class and working class. It also indicates that a large proportion of working class people will classify themselves as middle-class if the option is between being middle-class and lower-class.

One methodological issue here is whether self-identification is influenced primarily by the semantics of the answer options given, and therefore may not be related to the objective criteria of class. A plausible response to this doubt is that if the respondents were influenced by semantics, those who classified themselves as "middle-class" in the six-category class ladder would have continued to place themselves in the middle class, instead of switching to the working class, in the four-category class ladder. More importantly, there is evidence from comparative research elsewhere that "the link between objective class position and class identity tends to be strong" (Evans, 1994:127). Nevertheless, to strengthen the case for using subjective classes in our class map of Singapore, there is a need to determine whether the subjective classes have an objective basis.

This subjective class map of Singapore has turned out to be quite useful as it covers the entire sample, whereas the objective class maps (except for the ones based on total monthly household income and housing type) include only those who are currently working. Specifically, using occupational status as an indicator would mean that those who are not working, or almost half of the sample, will be left out of the analysis of class structure. To confirm our hunch that the four-category structure can serve as a comprehensive measure of class positions in Singapore, I have cross-tabulated positions on the four-category class structure by educational attainment, total monthly household income, and house-type (Tables 3.8, 3.9, and 3.10 respectively). All of these bivariate relationships are found to be statistically significant at $p = 0.000$, reflecting a high degree of correspondence between the objective and the subjective class indicators.

Table 3.8 Subjective class by educational attainment (per cent)

Class	Survey 2001	Educational Attainment					
		None	Pri.	Sec.	Post-sec.	Diploma	Degree
Upper	2	2	1	2	1	1	3
Middle	41	26	28	42	49	46	58
Working	51	56	59	51	48	50	39
Lower	6	16	13	5	1	3	0
Total ($N = 2248$)	100	100	100	100	100	100	100

Chi-square = 138.368, df = 15, $p = 0.000$ sig.

Table 3.9 Subjective class by monthly household income (per cent)

Class Survey 2001		Income Category			
		<$1000	$1000–2999	$3000–7999	$8000 and over
Upper	2	4	2	1	6
Middle	41	22	34	46	65
Working	51	46	57	52	29
Lower	6	28	8	1	0
Total (N = 2247)	100	100	100	100	100

Chi-square = 290.798, df = 9, $p = 0.000$ sig.

Table 3.10 Subjective class by house-type (per cent)

Class Survey 2001		House-type			
		One to three room	Four-room	Five room and executive	Private condo and landed
Upper	2	2	2	1	4
Middle	41	29	37	49	78
Working	51	55	57	49	18
Lower	6	14	4	1	1
Total (N = 2242)	100	100	100	100	100

Chi-square = 255.246, df = 9, $p = 0.000$ sig.

Nevertheless, where appropriate, I shall use several indicators of class as independent variables in the analysis chapters.

Class by age and ethnicity

This section focuses on the analysis of the four-category class structure by age and ethnicity. Table 3.11 shows that proportionally more of the younger working Singaporeans are found in the higher status occupations. This is not surprising, given that a larger proportion of younger Singaporeans have obtained higher qualifications. Table 3.11 can also be understood in terms of social mobility. It provides a

Table 3.11 Occupational status by age (per cent)

Occupational status	Survey 2001	Age category (years)			
		15–29	30–44	45–59	60–64
Service	48	58	50	41	19
Intermediate	26	32	26	22	25
Working	26	10	24	37	56
Total (N = 1455)	100	100	100	100	100

Chi-square = 95.081, df = 6, p = 0.000 sig.

Table 3.12 Subjective class by age (per cent)

Class	Survey 2001	Age category (years)			
		15–29	30–44	45–59	60–64
Upper	2	1	3	2	0
Middle	41	47	40	37	41
Working	51	49	53	53	44
Lower	6	3	5	9	16
Total (N = 2247)	100	100	100	100	100

Chi-square = 51.547, df = 9, p = 0.000 sig.

sense of the extent of upward occupational mobility between age cohorts and generations. When analyzed in terms of the four-category class structure (Table 3.12), the mobility pattern is somewhat less distinct, though it can be observed that 47 per cent of those aged 15–29 years identified themselves as middle class, as compared to 37 per cent of those aged 45–59 years, while 16 per cent of those aged 60–64 years placed themselves in the lower class, as compared to 3 per cent of those in the 15–29 age category.

With the prominence given to ethnicity in Singapore, it makes sense to gauge the extent of ethnic stratification in Singapore. Both Census 2000 and our survey indicate that proportionally more of the majority Chinese are in the service class as compared to their Malay or Indian counterparts (Table 3.13). However, and most interestingly, in regard to subjective class-identification, our data indicate that the class profiles of the four ethnic categories are statistically

18 Does Class Matter?

Table 3.13 Occupational status by ethnicity (per cent)

Occupational Status	Survey 2001	Ethnicity							
		Chinese		Malay		Indian		Others	
		S2001	C2000	S2001	C2000	S2001	C2000	S2001	C2000
Service	48	51	47	32	24	43	38	47	51
Intermediate	26	25	27	29	37	31	34	32	34
Working	26	24	26	39	39	26	28	21	15
Total ($N=1455$)	100	100	100	100	100	100	100	100	100

Chi-square = 28.585, df = 6, $p = 0.000$ sig.

Table 3.14 Subjective Class by Ethnicity (per cent)

Class	Survey 2001	Ethnicity			
		Chinese	Malay	Indian	Others
Upper	2	2	2	4	0
Middle	41	41	42	46	43
Working	51	52	50	44	54
Lower	6	6	6	6	4
Total (N=2247)	100	100	100	100	100

Chi-square=8.879, df=9, p=0.448 ns.

quite similar to one another, which means that the subjective ethnic stratification map is not characterized by ethnic inequality (Table 3.14). This perhaps reflects that the minorities are somewhat more inclined to see themselves as middle-class. If there is any validity to this observation, the picture that emerged here augurs well for ethnic relations in Singapore.

4

Social Orientations by Class, Age, and Ethnicity

How do Singaporeans differ from one another in terms of their social orientations? Are these differences related to class, ethnicity, and age? The term "social orientations" is defined here in a broad sense to include the economic and political dimensions as well. The rationale for focusing on age as an independent variable is to obtain a sense of the extent of inter-generational changes, while class and ethnicity provide some indication of the kind of tension and variation in outlook that may have their source in social inequality. To situate our findings on social orientations within the current context characterized by recession, we will begin by examining the reported household budget situation.

Reported household budget situation

Table 4.1 shows that most Singaporean households (82 per cent) are reportedly living within their means at least in the early half of 2001. It can also be observed that household budgets are less likely to be balanced down the class ladder (Table 4.2), and that the reported budget profiles of the various ethnic categories are not statistically

Table 4.1 Reported Household budget situation by ethnicity (per cent)

Reported household budget situation	Survey 2001	Ethnicity			
		Chinese	Malay	Indian	Others
Income more than expenditure	29	30	26	32	32
Income = expenditure	53	53	55	52	50
Income less than expenditure	17	17	19	16	18
Total	100	100	100	100	100

Chi-square = 2.984, df = 6, p = 0.811 ns.

Table 4.2 Reported household budget situation by class (per cent)

Reported household budget situation	Class			
	Upper	Middle	Working	Lower
Income more than expenditure	41	34	27	13
Income = expenditure	52	52	55	46
Income less than expenditure	7	14	17	41
Total	100	100	100	100

Chi-square = 75.576, df = 6, p = 0.000 sig.

different from one another (Table 4.1). These figures indicate that unbalanced household budget situation is more of a class, rather than ethnic, phenomenon. They also suggest that the middle class and working class experienced almost similar budget situation during the previous three months, while two out of five persons from the lower class reported a household budget deficit (Table 4.2).

Success factors

As noted earlier, Singapore practises a policy of equality of opportunity and meritocracy. In itself, this does not mean the absence of class reproduction, whether as an objective outcome or as part of subjective consciousness. A relevant question to ask is whether Singaporeans think of success as dependent on individual ability and effort, or on social connection, which is a function of social class, or on luck, a random factor not within anybody's control.

Table 4.3 indicates that, on a scale of 1–5, where 1 means "most important" and 5 means "least important", education was rated the most important (1.83), while social connection and luck were perceived to be of lower importance (3.71 and 4.33 respectively). Table 4.3 also reveals an interesting pattern: in relative terms, the elderly believe in hard work; middle-age people point to education; those in the midst of building their careers give more weightage to connection and luck; while younger Singaporeans attribute success to ability. This pattern is reflective of the social experience of the different age cohorts.

The analysis by ethnicity and class reveals equally fascinating patterns as well. For instance, the Chinese are, as compared to the non-Chinese, relatively more likely to consider "luck" as important. This finding resonates with a common stereotype image of the Chinese as gamblers (Table 4.4).

In terms of class, the data indicate that the middle and working class are, in relative terms, more likely to emphasize "ability" and

Table 4.3 Success factors by age (mean score), where 1 = most important, 5 = least important

Attribute	Survey 2001	Age category* (years)			
		15–29	30–44	45–59	60–64
Ability	2.60	2.43	2.72	2.60	2.56
Education	1.83	1.84	1.91	1.70	1.88
Hard work	2.53	2.64	2.52	2.45	2.36
Connection	3.71	3.65	3.64	3.86	3.88
Luck	4.33	4.44	4.21	4.39	4.33

*$p \leq 0.05$.

Table 4.4 Success factors by ethnicity (mean score), where 1 = most important, 5 = least important

Attribute	Ethnicity*			
	Chinese	Malay	Indian	Others
Ability	2.57	2.62	2.79	2.75
Education	1.90	1.59	1.56	1.48
Hard work	2.59	2.26	2.38	2.50
Connection	3.69	3.87	3.75	3.64
Luck	4.25	4.66	4.52	4.62

*$p \leq 0.05$ sig.

Table 4.5 Success factors by class (mean score), where 1 = most important, 5 = least important

Attribute	Class*			
	Upper	**Middle**	**Working**	**Lower**
Ability	2.77	2.51	2.63	2.84
Education	2.11	1.87	1.78	1.93
Hard work	2.59	2.49	2.57	2.41
Connection	3.44	3.66	3.77	3.74
Luck	4.08	4.47	4.27	4.07

*$p \leq 0.05$ sig., except for "hard work".

"education", while the lower class show a greater inclination to subscribe to "luck" (Table 4.5). Interestingly, apart from attributing success to "social connection", the upper class are just as likely as the lower class to stress the importance of "luck" as a success factor. This finding differs partially from that of the 1983 study of Quah et al. (1991). They found that those in high prestige occupations are more likely to believe in "luck" as a success factor than those in low prestige occupations (Quah et al., 1991). They explained that those in "high prestige occupations are typically high income earners and better educated than the rest; their knowledge and their own experience moving (or struggling) to the top may have taught them that luck is part of the process of advancement...(while) people in low prestige jobs which generate low income and only require lower than average education, may centre their hopes in the social system of rewards that promises success for hard work" (Quah et al., 1991:101). However, it may be argued, on the basis of our finding here, that, even as the lower class think of "hard work" as giving them hope for upward mobility, their seeing "luck" as a success factor makes it easier for them to accept their lack of success.

While we have highlighted the statistically significant differences between age, class, and ethnic categories above, it should be noted that, by and large, Singaporeans, regardless of age, class, and ethnicity, tend to give similar rankings to the five attributes. This suggests some convergence or homogeneity in their orientations towards success values.

Singapore: a land of opportunity for everyone?

Corresponding to the above findings that education, hard work, and ability are deemed to be the more important factors for achieving success, we found that close to 80 percent of Singaporeans perceive Singapore to be a land of opportunity for achieving a high standard of living (Table 4.6). Younger Singaporeans are somewhat more inclined to think so, probably a reflection of their possessing higher educational qualifications (Table 4.6). In terms of ethnicity, the Malays are somewhat more likely to agree that Singapore is a land of opportunity (Table 4.7). If this finding has any validity, it augurs

Table 4.6 "Everyone in Singapore has a good chance to achieve a high standard of living" by age (per cent)

"Everyone in Singapore has a good chance to achieve a high standard of living"	Survey 2001	Age category (years)			
		15–29	30–44	45–59	60–64
Agree	78	82	77	77	77
Neutral	4	4	3	5	5
Disagree	18	14	20	19	18
Total	100	100	100	100	100

Chi-square = 12.988, df = 6, $p = 0.043$ sig.

Table 4.7 "Everyone in Singapore has a good chance to achieve a high standard of living" by ethnicity (per cent)

"Everyone in Singapore has a good chance to achieve a high standard of living"	Ethnicity			
	Chinese	Malay	Indian	Others
Agree	77	86	77	72
Neutral	4	4	5	3
Disagree	19	10	19	24
Total	100	100	100	100

Chi-square = 13.531, df = 6, $p = 0.035$ sig.

Table 4.8 "Everyone in Singapore has a good chance to achieve a high standard of living" by class (per cent)

"Everyone in Singapore has a good chance to achieve a high standard of living"	Class			
	Upper	Middle	Working	Lower
Agree	74	82	77	65
Neutral	0	3	4	10
Disagree	26	15	18	25
Total	100	100	100	100

Chi-square = 28.639, df = 6, p = 0.000 sig.

well for ethnic relations in Singapore. Interestingly, the pattern in terms of class is an inverse-U shape with the middle and working class more likely to think of Singapore as a land of opportunity (Table 4.8). As noted above, "social connection" and "luck" seem to be relatively more important to the upper class, even as "luck" features somewhat more prominently among the lower class. However, for the middle and working class, it is plausible that their emphasis on ability and education resonates with their perception of Singapore as a land of opportunity.

Orientation towards state welfarism

While a large majority of Singaporeans think of Singapore as a land of opportunity where individual ability and effort count in achieving success, this did not stop them from supporting some form of welfarism for the poor. In relative terms, older Singaporeans are somewhat more likely to support welfarism for the poor. Perhaps, this stems from the fact that they are likely to have less education, less resources, and, more importantly, to be in the "consumption" phase of the life-cycle (Table 4.9). Tables 4.10 and 4.11 indicate that support for state welfarism is more of an age phenomenon than a class or ethnic phenomenon.

Table 4.9 "The government should give financial assistance to the poor" by age (per cent)

"The government should give financial assistance to the poor"	Survey 2001	Age category (years)			
		15–29	30–44	45–59	60–64
Agree	95	95	95	96	98
Neutral	3	5	2	2	0
Disagree	2	1	3	2	2
Total	100	100	100	100	100

Chi-square = 23.558, df = 6, p = 0.001 sig.

Table 4.10 "The government should give financial assistance to the poor" by ethnicity (per cent)

"The government should give financial assistance to the poor"	Ethnicity			
	Chinese	Malay	Indian	Others
Agree	95	97	97	96
Neutral	3	1	1	4
Disagree	2	2	2	0
Total	100	100	100	100

Chi-square = 9.292, df = 6, p = 0.158 ns.

Table 4.11 "The government should give financial assistance to the poor" by class (per cent)

"The government should give financial assistance to the poor"	Class			
	Upper	Middle	Working	Lower
Agree	91	95	95	99
Neutral	5	3	3	0
Disagree	5	2	2	1
Total	100	100	100	100

Chi-square = 7.833, df = 6, p = 0.251 ns.

Orientation towards community support

Somewhat similar to the support for state welfarism, a large majority of Singaporeans believe that successful people have a responsibility to help the less successful ones in their midst (Table 4.12). Here again, older Singaporeans are more likely to hold this view (Table 4.12). Another observation is that the Malays have a greater likelihood to agree that successful people should help the less successful ones (Table 4.13). Like the item on state welfarism, orientation towards community support is not a class phenomenon (Table 4.14).

Table 4.12 "People who are more successful have a responsibility to help the less successful ones" by age (per cent)

"People who are more successful have a responsibility to help the less successful ones"	Survey 2001	Age category (years)			
		15–29	30–44	45–59	60–64
Agree	87	86	83	92	93
Neutral	5	8	4	3	2
Disagree	8	6	13	6	5
Total	100	100	100	100	100

Chi-square = 57.202, df = 6, $p = 0.000$ sig.

Table 4.13 "People who are more successful have a responsibility to help the less successful ones" by ethnicity (per cent)

"People who are more successful have a responsibility to help the less successful ones"	Ethnicity			
	Chinese	Malay	Indian	Others
Agree	86	94	87	89
Neutral	5	2	6	4
Disagree	9	4	7	7
Total	100	100	100	100

Chi-square = 16.677, df = 6, $p = 0.011$ sig.

Table 4.14 "People who are more successful have a responsibility to help the less successful ones" by class (per cent)

"People who are more successful have a responsibility to help the less successful ones"	Class			
	Upper	Middle	Working	Lower
Agree	95	87	87	90
Neutral	0	5	5	3
Disagree	5	8	9	7
Total	100	100	100	100

Chi-square = 5.033, df = 6, p = 0.540 ns.

Support for unionism

It should not be surprising that support for unionism is related to class, since unions are originally, if not primarily, working class organizations. Tables 4.15–4.18 present results for the view "working people in Singapore should join unions" in relation to occupational status, class, age, and ethnicity, respectively, while Tables 4.19–4.22 show the corresponding results for the view "Singapore unions ensure that their members are treated fairly". Tables 4.15 and 4.19 indicate that those in the working class occupational category are more likely to support unionism than their service or intermediate class counterparts in the labour force. Interestingly, when analysed in terms of the subjective class categories, while the working class (61 per cent) are, as expected, more likely to be supportive of unionism, it can be observed that 59 percent of the self-identified upper class are just as likely to agree that "Working people in Singapore should join unions" (Table 4.16). A plausible explanation for the latter finding is that the self-identified upper class may have, in their work experience as managers or proprietors, observed that unions do provide some protection to workers. Indeed, Table 4.20 indicates that the self-identified upper class are somewhat more likely than the other class categories to hold the view that "Singapore unions ensure that their members are treated fairly".

With regards to age (Tables 4.17 and 4.21), I suspect that the weaker support for unionism among younger Singaporeans stems

Table 4.15 "Working people in Singapore should join unions" by occupational status (per cent)

"Working people in Singapore should join unions"	Survey 2001	Occupational status		
		Service	Intermediate	Working
Agree	60	57	61	65
Neutral	17	17	20	14
Disagree	23	26	19	22
Total	100	100	100	100

Chi-square = 11.826, df = 4, p = 0.019 sig.

Table 4.16 "Working people in Singapore should join unions" by Class (per cent)

"Working people in Singapore should join unions"	Class			
	Upper	Middle	Working	Lower
Agree	59	56	61	59
Neutral	10	23	16	26
Disagree	31	21	24	15
Total	100	100	100	100

Chi-square = 23.313, df = 6, p = 0.001 sig.

Table 4.17 "Working people in Singapore should join unions" by age (per cent)

"Working people in Singapore should join unions"	Survey 2001	Age category (years)			
		15–29	30–44	45–59	60–64
Agree	59	40	63	70	68
Neutral	19	32	15	13	13
Disagree	22	27	22	18	19
Total	100	100	100	100	100

Chi-square = 143.363, df = 6, p = 0.000 sig.

from their possessing higher educational qualifications and thereby an orientation towards service or intermediate occupational status jobs, precisely the categories that are more inclined towards thinking of job benefits as "dependent on individual performance and

Table 4.18 "Working people in Singapore should join unions" by ethnicity (per cent)

"Working people in Singapore should join unions"	Ethnicity			
	Chinese	Malay	Indian	Others
Agree	57	67	60	59
Neutral	21	15	16	11
Disagree	23	18	25	30
Total	100	100	100	100

Chi-square = 14.763, df = 6, p = 0.022 sig.

Table 4.19 "Singapore unions ensure that their members are treated fairly" by occupational status (per cent)

"Singapore unions ensure that their members are treated fairly"	Survey 2001	Occupational status		
		Service	Intermediate	Working
Agree	60	57	61	65
Neutral	17	18	20	14
Disagree	23	26	19	22
Total	100	100	100	100

Chi-square = 11.826, df = 4, p = 0.019 sig.

Table 4.20 "Singapore unions ensure that their members are treated fairly" by class (per cent)

"Singapore unions ensure that their members are treated fairly"	Class			
	Upper	Middle	Working	Lower
Agree	67	63	66	59
Neutral	17	23	14	29
Disagree	17	14	20	13
Total	100	100	100	100

Chi-square = 43.272, df = 6, p = 0.000 sig.

Table 4.21 "Singapore unions ensure that their members are treated fairly" by age (per cent)

"Singapore unions ensure that their members are treated fairly"	Survey 2001	Age category (years)			
		15–29	30–44	45–59	60–64
Agree	64	51	67	73	71
Neutral	19	27	16	12	19
Disagree	17	22	17	15	10
Total	100	100	100	100	100

Chi-square = 75.934, df = 6, p = 0.000 sig.

Table 4.22 "Singapore unions ensure that their members are treated fairly" by ethnicity (per cent)

"Singapore unions ensure that their members are treated fairly"	Ethnicity			
	Chinese	Malay	Indian	Others
Agree	63	70	62	63
Neutral	19	16	21	11
Disagree	18	14	18	26
Total	100	100	100	100

Chi-square = 7.831, df = 6, p = 0.251 ns.

professional expertise, rather than the collective power of worker organizations" (Tan, 2000:8). Another explanation is that a large proportion of those in the younger age category have not begun working life, let alone have personal contact with unions.

With regards to how unionism fare in terms of ethnicity, Table 4.18 shows that the minorities, especially the Malays, are more likely to be supportive of unionism. Table 4.22 provides some indication that the Malays are more likely to perceive that "Singapore unions ensure that their members are treated fairly". However, since the relationship between this unionism item and ethnicity is not statistically significant, it may be inferred that support for unionism is more of an age and class phenomenon, rather than an ethnic phenomenon.

Orientation towards political participation

Political participation is a key indicator and life-blood of democracy. It is facilitated by participation opportunity, a system characteristic, and participation propensity, a citizen characteristic. In this study, we use perceived participation opportunity as an approximate measure of participation opportunity. "Perceived participation opportunity" is defined as "the degree of influence which citizens *have* on national issues", while "participation propensity" is defined as "the degree of influence citizens *should have* on national issues". It is possible that some citizens have higher participation propensity than what they perceive the system allows, a condition which we shall term as "political alienation".

Unlike their relatively weak support for unionism, younger Singaporeans are more likely to have a "medium" or "high" propensity for political participation. However, because they also perceive that Singapore citizens have "a great deal" or "some" influence on national issues, the proportion among them that can be classified as "politically alienated" is lower than those in the middle age (45–59) category (Tables 4.23–4.25).

When analysed in terms of ethnicity, our data suggest that the minorities, in particular Indian Singaporeans, are more likely to have a high propensity for political participation (Table 4.26). However, because they are also more likely to perceive that there is a high degree of opportunity for participation (Table 4.27), it turns out that

Table 4.23 Participation propensity by age (per cent)

Participation propensity	Survey 2001	Age category (years)			
		15–29	30–44	45–59	60–64
High	13	13) 78	12) 65	15) 67	8) 52
Medium	56	65)	53)	52)	44)
Low	32	22	35	34	48
Total	100	100	100	100	100

Chi-square = 55.087, df = 6, $p = 0.000$ sig.

Table 4.24 Perceived participation opportunity by age (per cent)

Perceived participation opportunity	Survey 2001	Age category (years)			
		15–29	30–44	45–59	60–64
High	8	7 (62)	8 (51)	8 (48)	10 (45)
Medium	45	55	43	40	35
Low	47	38	50	52	55
Total	100	100	100	100	100

Chi-square = 43.404, df = 6, $p = 0.000$ sig.

Table 4.25 Political alienation score by age (per cent)

Political alienation score	Survey 2001	Age category (years)			
		15–29	30–44	45–59	60–64
Positive	23	22	21	26	16
Zero	73	75	75	69	72
Negative	4	3	4	5	12
Total	100	100	100	100	100

Chi-square = 29.341, df = 6, $p = 0.000$ sig.

Table 4.26 Participation propensity by ethnicity (per cent)

Participation propensity	Survey 2001	Ethnicity			
		Chinese	Malay	Indian	Others
High	13	11	16	24	11
Medium	56	55	57	55	68
Low	32	34	27	21	21
Total	100	100	100	100	100

Chi-square = 37.508, df = 6, $p = 0.000$ sig.

political alienation (as measured by the difference between participation propensity and perceived participation opportunity) is not an ethnic phenomenon (Table 4.28).

In contrast with the analysis in terms of ethnicity, political alienation appears to be a class phenomenon. The relevant figures suggest that the upper and middle class are more likely to have a

Table 4.27 Perceived participation opportunity by ethnicity (per cent)

Perceived participation opportunity	Survey 2001	Ethnicity			
		Chinese	Malay	Indian	Others
High	8	7	11	15	7
Medium	45	44	50	49	54
Low	47	50	39	36	39
Total	100	100	100	100	100

Chi-square = 36.721, df = 6, p = 0.000 sig.

Table 4.28 Political alienation score by ethnicity (per cent)

Political alienation score	Survey 2001	Ethnicity			
		Chinese	Malay	Indian	Others
Positive	23	23	19	23	22
Zero	73	73	76	73	74
Negative	4	4	4	4	4
Total	100	100	100	100	100

Chi-square = 2.131, df = 6, p = 0.907 ns.

Table 4.29 Participation propensity by class (per cent)

Participation propensity	Survey 2001	Class			
		Upper	Middle	Working	Lower
High	13	21	15	11	11
Medium	56	59	58	56	40
Low	32	21	28	33	49
Total	100	100	100	100	100

Chi-square = 34.388, df = 6, p = 0.000 sig.

high participation propensity (Table 4.29), but once perceived participation opportunity (Table 4.30) is taken into consideration, Tables 4.31 and 4.32 show that the middle class are the least politically alienated, while the upper class remain in the lead, followed by the working and lower class. The finding that people in the middle class possess a high participation propensity is not surprising, given that they are usually hypothesized to be the most vocal in

Table 4.30 Perceived participation opportunity by class (per cent)

Perceived participation opportunity	Survey 2001	Class			
		Upper	Middle	Working	Lower
High	8	16	10	6	4
Medium	45	30	50	43	31
Low	47	54	39	51	65
Total	100	100	100	100	100

Chi-square = 59.062, df = 6, p = 0.000 sig.

Table 4.31 Political alienation score by class (per cent)

Political alienation score	Survey 2001	Class			
		Upper	Middle	Working	Lower
Positive	23	35	19	25	24
Zero	73	61	76	72	73
Negative	4	5	5	4	3
Total	100	100	100	100	100

Chi-square = 14.574, df = 6, p = 0.024 sig.

Table 4.32 Political alienation score by class (mean score)

Class	Mean score Scale − 1 to + 1, where 1 = high
Upper	0.30
Middle	0.14
Working	0.21
Lower	0.21
Total sample	0.18

demanding for "both a share in political power, and also a shift in the nature of that power" (Jones and Brown, 1994:80).

However, Jones and Brown (1994:80) have argued that the middle class in Singapore, unlike their counterparts in the West, are not inclined towards liberal democracy, but have a tendency to conform and a desire for strong, good government. By the same token, Mak (1997:14–15) maintained that "proactive politics is found to be wanting among (the) middle classes (in Singapore)". Moreover, while both Jones and Brown (1994) and Mak (1997) would agree that the Singapore middle class is not politically alienated, they would attribute this to the middle class' dependence on the government for beneficial policies and for direction. Mak (1997:15) further suggested that "the (middle class') feeling of not having viable channels for political expression serves as a check on their political enthusiasm". In contrast, our data indicate that the middle class scores high on participation propensity, matched by high perceived participation opportunity, thereby resulting in a low score on political alienation.

Cross-class ties

This section focuses on some data that hint at the potential for inter-class tension. Tables 4.33 and 4.34 suggest that cross-class friendships tend to be asymmetrical. While the higher classes have "lower income" friends, the lower classes are less likely to have "higher income" friends. Moreover, as one moves down the class ladder, one would find proportionally more people saying that "successful people in Singapore tend to look down on the less successful ones" (Table 4.35).

Cross-ethnic ties

On the dimension of cross-ethnic ties, we found that younger Singaporeans, minorities, and middle class Singaporeans are more

Table 4.33 "Have friends from lower income groups" by class (per cent)

"Have friends from lower income groups"	Survey 2001	Class			
		Upper	Middle	Working	Lower
Agree	85	83	85	86	83
Neutral	4	5	4	4	7
Disagree	11	12	11	11	11
Total	100	100	100	100	100

Chi-square = 2.371, df = 6, p = 0.883 ns.

Table 4.34 "Have friends from higher income groups" by class (per cent)

"Have friends from higher income groups"	Survey 2001	Class			
		Upper	Middle	Working	Lower
Agree	77	79	84	74	54
Neutral	5	5	4	6	6
Disagree	18	17	12	20	41
Total	100	100	100	100	100

Chi-square = 75.406, df = 6, p = 0.000 sig.

Table 4.35 "Successful people in Singapore tend to look down on the less successful ones" by class (per cent)

"Successful people in Singapore tend to look down on the less successful ones"	Survey 2001	Class			
		Upper	Middle	Working	Lower
Agree	47	44	41	50	60
Neutral	10	2	12	10	5
Disagree	43	54	47	40	36
Total	100	100	100	100	100

Chi-square = 75.406, df = 6, p = 0.000 sig.

likely to have "close friends of a different race" (Tables 4.36–4.38). A plausible explanation for the age factor is that younger Singaporeans may be more exposed to "racial harmony" messages, and have more opportunity to interact across ethnic lines. As for why minorities are more likely to have close friends across ethnic lines, I have elsewhere argued that being numerically smaller means that they are more likely to "bump into" people of a different race than themselves. In regard to the extent of cross-ethnic ties being a class phenomenon, it could be that people in the lower class, who are likely to have low education, have a higher tendency to be ethnocentric, which in turn renders close friendship across ethnic lines less likely (cf. Brown, 1965:522; Rempel and Clark, 1997:21). Indeed,

Table 4.36 "Have close friends of a different race" by age (per cent)

"Have close friends of a different race"	Survey 2001	Age category (years)			
		15–29	30–44	45–59	60–64
Agree	75	83	74	70	68
Neutral	4	6	3	2	3
Disagree	21	10	23	29	30
Total	100	100	100	100	100

Chi-square = 86.303, df = 6, p = 0.000 sig.

Table 4.37 "Have close friends of a different race" by ethnicity (per cent)

"Have close friends of a different race"	Ethnicity			
	Chinese	Malay	Indian	Others
Agree	70	90	91	89
Neutral	4	1	2	0
Disagree	25	9	6	11
Total	100	100	100	100

Chi-square = 84.473, df = 6, p = 0.000 sig.

Table 4.38 "Have close friends of a different race" by class (per cent)

"Have close friends of a different race"	Class			
	Upper	Middle	Working	Lower
Agree	72	78	74	65
Neutral	5	5	3	1
Disagree	23	17	23	34
Total	100	100	100	100

Chi-square = 28.516, df = 6, p = 0.000 sig.

Table 4.39 provides a strong indication that, as compared to their counterparts with secondary or higher education, Singaporeans with primary or lower education are less likely to have "close friends of a different race".

Table 4.39 "Have close friends of a different race" by education (per cent)

"Have close friends of a different race"	Education level			
	Pri. or lower	Sec.	Post-sec.	Univ. or prof.
Agree	63	79	77	77
Neutral	2	3	7	5
Disagree	35	18	15	18
Total	100	100	100	100

Chi-square = 97.982, df = 6, p = 0.000 sig.

Orientation towards Singapore—the nation and economy

Apart from examining the orientations of Singaporeans towards cross-class and cross-ethnic ties, this study analyses their orientations towards Singapore—the nation and economy. The overall picture that emerged from the analysis shows that national pride is rather strong, with 94 percent of the sample agreeing that they are proud to be Singaporeans (Table 4.40).

With regards to specific aspects of Singapore, young Singaporeans are somewhat more inclined to take a neutral stand when asked if they thought Singapore has "more good points than bad points", if it is "a good place to make a living", or if it is "a good place to raise one's children" (Tables 4.41, 4.44, and 4.47). The complete results with regards to age, ethnicity, and class are presented in Tables 4.41–4.49. Furthermore, only 64 percent of young Singaporeans thought of Singapore as "a good place to make a living", compared to 75 percent in the case of their counterparts in the 45–59 age category (Table 4.44). Perhaps, the almost back-to-back recession in recent years has had a more poignant effect on how young Singaporeans view their economic prospects in Singapore. Indeed, the proportion of young Singaporeans who perceived Singapore to be *not* "a good place to make a living" is above the sample mean (Table 4.44).

As with several other aspects analysed in this chapter, ethnicity does not have a statistically significant impact on how Singaporeans

Table 4.40 Distribution of "I am proud to be a Singaporean" (per cent)

"I am proud to be a Singaporean"	Percent
Strongly agree	26) 94
Agree	68)
Neutral	3
Disagree	3
Strongly disagree	0
Total	100

Table 4.41 "Singapore has more good points than bad points" by age (per cent)

"Singapore has more good points than bad points"	Survey 2001	Age category (years)			
		15–29	30–44	45–59	60–64
Agree	85	84	86	85	82
Neutral	10	14	8	8	9
Disagree	5	2	6	6	9
Total	100	100	100	100	100

Chi-square = 32.620, df = 6, p = 0.000 sig.

Table 4.42 "Singapore has more good points than bad points" by ethnicity (per cent)

"Singapore has more good points than bad points"	Ethnicity			
	Chinese	Malay	Indian	Others
Agree	84	89	86	86
Neutral	11	8	9	7
Disagree	5	3	5	7
Total	100	100	100	100

Chi-square = 5.766, df = 6, p = 0.450 ns.

view Singapore (Tables 4.42 and 4.48). A three-way analysis of variance (ANOVA) with each of the above three "orientation towards Singapore" items as dependent variables and ethnicity, age, and class as independent variables provides further confirmation that

Table 4.43 "Singapore has more good points than bad points" by class (per cent)

"Singapore has more good points than bad points"	Class			
	Upper	Middle	Working	Lower
Agree	86	87	85	72
Neutral	5	8	10	21
Disagree	9	5	5	7
Total	100	100	100	100

Chi-square = 26.172, df = 6, p = 0.000 sig.

Table 4.44 "Singapore is a good place to make a living" by age (per cent)

"Singapore is a good place to make a living"	Survey 2001	Age category (years)			
		15–29	30–44	45–59	60–64
Agree	69	64	69	75	66
Neutral	8	10	8	6	10
Disagree	23	26	23	19	24
Total	100	100	100	100	100

Chi-square = 19.913, df = 6, p = 0.003 sig.

Table 4.45 "Singapore is a good place to make a living" by ethnicity (per cent)

"Singapore is a good place to make a living"	Ethnicity			
	Chinese	Malay	Indian	Others
Agree	68	77	74	68
Neutral	8	6	9	4
Disagree	24	17	18	29
Total	100	100	100	100

Chi-square = 15.216, df = 6, p = 0.019 sig.

ethnicity does not have a statistically significant impact on how Singaporeans perceive Singapore.[3]

In contrast, class does seem to matter. More specifically, the middle class as a category has consistently scored the highest in terms of overall life satisfaction and orientation towards Singapore, understood as "having more good points than bad points", "a good place to make a living", and "a good place to raise children" (Tables 4.43, 4.46, and 4.49). A plausible explanation for this finding is that the middle class has experienced substantial improvement in living standard and upward social mobility over the last three decades. This reflects well on the government's economic policies and has enhanced its political legitimacy. However, with the current recession and the advent of the "new insecurity" (noted in Chapter 1),

Table 4.46 "Singapore is a good place to make a living" by class (per cent)

"Singapore is a good place to make a living"	Class			
	Upper	**Middle**	**Working**	**Lower**
Agree	71	73	67	65
Neutral	3	7	8	14
Disagree	26	20	25	21
Total	100	100	100	100

Chi-square = 17.458, df = 6, p = 0.008 sig.

Table 4.47 "Singapore is a good place to raise one's children" by age (per cent)

"Singapore is a good place to raise one's children"	Survey 2001	Age category (years)			
		15–29	30–44	45–59	60–64
Agree	78	77	77	78	81
Neutral	7	12	6	5	3
Disagree	15	10	17	16	17
Total	100	100	100	100	100

Chi-square = 46.359, df = 6, p = 0.000 sig.

---

[3] The SPSS-procedure for distilling the effects of class, age, and ethnicity is as follows: Analyse-General Linear Model-Univariate.

Table 4.48 "Singapore is a good place to raise one's children" by ethnicity (per cent)

"Singapore is a good place to raise one's children"	Ethnicity			
	Chinese	Malay	Indian	Others
Agree	77	83	78	79
Neutral	8	5	9	7
Disagree	15	12	13	14
Total	100	100	100	100

Chi-square = 7.173, df = 6, p = 0.305 ns.

Table 4.49 "Singapore is a good place to raise one's children" by class (per cent)

"Singapore is a good place to raise one's children"	Class			
	Upper	Middle	Working	Lower
Agree	67	81	76	77
Neutral	2	6	8	12
Disagree	30	13	16	11
Total	100	100	100	100

Chi-square = 22.425, df = 6, p = 0.001 sig.

there is a likelihood that the scores on these three variables may decline in the near future. But this is not a foregone conclusion, if Singapore succeeds in re-inventing its economy.

Overall life satisfaction

To capture a generic dimension, the respondents were asked to rate their overall life satisfaction. Table 4.50 suggests that 86 percent of Singaporeans are either "very satisfied" or "satisfied". Young Singaporeans are somewhat less satisfied with life, perhaps a reflection of their higher expectations or perception of the current economic situation. As before, ethnicity does not appear to affect overall life satisfaction (Table 4.51). The pattern for class as independent variable is an inverse-U shape, with the middle and working class more likely to express overall satisfaction with life (Table 4.52).

Table 4.50 Overall life satisfaction by age (per cent)

Overall life satisfaction	Survey 2001	Age category (years)			
		15–29	30–44	45–59	60–64
Very satisfied	10	10	9	10	15
Satisfied	76	72	78	78	74
Not satisfied	13	17	11	11	10
Not satisfied at all	1	1	2	1	1
Total	100	100	100	100	100

Chi-square = 22.822, df = 9, p = 0.007 sig.

Table 4.51 Overall life satisfaction by ethnicity (per cent)

Overall life satisfaction	Ethnicity			
	Chinese	Malay	Indian	Others
Very satisfied	10	12	12	11
Satisfied	76	76	74	78
Not satisfied	13	11	13	11
Not satisfied at all	1	1	1	0
Total	100	100	100	100

Chi-square = 3.728, df = 9, p = 0.928 ns.

Table 4.52 Overall life satisfaction by class (per cent)

Overall life satisfaction	Class			
	Upper	Middle	Working	Lower
Very satisfied	9	15	7	4
Satisfied	67	77	78	56
Not satisfied	23	8	13	34
Not satisfied at all	0	0	2	6
Total	100	100	100	100

Chi-square = 138.058, df = 9, p = 0.000 sig.

Extent of optimism

How do Singaporeans view the future? Paradoxically, while young Singaporeans (Table 4.53) and the upper class (Table 4.55) were less upbeat on the previous items, they seem to express greater optimism about the near future. (Tables 4.53–4.55 present the results with

Table 4.53 Perceived financial situation over the next 5 years by age (per cent)

Perceived financial situation over the next 5 years	Survey 2001	Age category (years)			
		15–29	30–44	45–59	60–64
Better than now	33	53	29	20	11
About the same as now	58	44	61	66	71
Worse than now	10	3	10	14	18
Total	100	100	100	100	100

Chi-square = 220.724, df = 6, $p = 0.000$ sig.

Table 4.54 Perceived financial situation over the next 5 years by ethnicity (per cent)

Perceived financial situation over the next 5 years	Ethnicity			
	Chinese	Malay	Indian	Others
Better than now	30	40	41	41
About the same as now	59	53	51	52
Worse than now	10	7	8	7
Total	100	100	100	100

Chi-square = 21.680 df = 6, $p = 0.001$ sig.

Table 4.55 Perceived financial situation over the next 5 years by class (per cent)

Perceived financial situation over the next 5 years	Class			
	Upper	Middle	Working	Lower
Better than now	56	40	29	13
About the same as now	42	55	61	58
Worse than now	2	6	11	29
Total	100	100	100	100

Chi-square = 115.696 df = 6, $p = 0.00$ sig.

regard to age, ethnicity, and class, respectively.) This suggests a more stable orientation on the part of middle age and middle class Singaporeans. It could also be that the earlier items—perceptions about whether Singapore is "a good place to raise children" and "a good place to make a living"—deal with a more deep-seated belief, and are therefore not easily influenced by economic fluctuations. With regard to ethnicity, Table 4.54 shows that, as compared to the majority Chinese, the minorities are more likely to feel optimistic about the near future. This provides another indication of the healthy ethnic relations climate in Singapore.

5

Work Career and Social Mobility

This chapter focuses on work career and social mobility, two aspects of class dynamics, to get a sense of the extent to which Singaporeans are moving up the social ladder and whether or not they are likely to pursue skills upgrading or professional development as part of their career strategies. We shall first consider how those currently working view their business or career prospects.

Business and career prospects

Of those involved in business ($N=186$), close to three-fourths perceive their business prospects to be "average" or better, including 13 per cent who are upbeat (Table 5.1).

The perceived situation is even more buoyant among those in employment, with close to a third indicating "good" or "very good" when asked to rate their career prospects over the next 5 years (Table 5.2). Tables 5.2–5.5 show a statistically significant relationship between perceived career prospects and age, occupational status, and class, respectively, but not ethnicity. Young Singaporeans and those in high status jobs are likely to be more optimistic about their

Table 5.1 Perceived business prospects over the next 5 years (per cent)

Perceived business prospects	Per cent
Very good	2) 13
Good	11)
Average	60
Poor	22) 23
Very poor	1)
NA	4
Total ($N=186$)	100

Table 5.2 Perceived career prospects over the next 5 years by age (per cent)

Perceived career prospects	Survey 2001	Age category (years)			
		15–29	30–44	45–59	60–64
Very good/good	32	42	34	21	8
Average	48	42	50	49	67
Very poor/poor	20	16	16	30	26
Total ($N=1227$)	100	100	100	100	100

Chi-square = 57.137, df = 6, $p=0.000$ sig.

Table 5.3 Perceived career prospects over the next 5 years by ethnicity (per cent)

Perceived career prospects	Ethnicity			
	Chinese	Malay	Indian	Others
Very good/good	30	39	35	40
Average	49	46	49	53
Very poor/poor	22	15	16	7
Total ($N=1228$)	100	100	100	100

Chi-square = 10.776, df = 6, $p=0.096$ ns.

Table 5.4 Perceived career prospects over the next 5 years by occupational status (per cent)

Perceived career prospects	Occupational status		
	Service	Intermediate	Working
Very good/good	46	30	12
Average	45	54	48
Very poor/poor	10	17	40
Total ($N = 1228$)	100	100	100

Chi-square = 175.433, df = 4, $p = 0.000$ sig.

Table 5.5 Perceived career prospects over the next 5 years by class (per cent)

Perceived career prospects	Class			
	Upper	Middle	Working	Lower
Very good/good	68	43	26	6
Average	26	46	52	33
Very poor/poor	5	11	23	60
Total ($N = 1228$)	100	100	100	100

Chi-square = 130.232, df = 6, $p = 0.000$ sig.

future career prospects. One may argue, positively, that this reflects their confidence in or, negatively, their unrealistic assessment of the future. In contrast, 60 per cent of the self-identified lower-class felt that their future career prospects were poor. These findings are in the expected direction.

Skills upgrading prospects

The findings on perceived prospects of skills upgrading or professional development are rather similar to that of perceived career prospects (Tables 5.6–5.9). This is not surprising, given that skills upgrading and career prospects are logically related to one another. It is noteworthy that minority Singaporeans are somewhat more optimistic about skills upgrading or professional development than their Chinese counterparts; and that where ethnicity does matter, its impact is in the positive direction (Table 5.7).

Table 5.6 Prospects of skills upgrading or professional development over the next 5 years by age (per cent)

Perceived upgrading prospects	Survey 2001	Age category (years)			
		15–29	30–44	45–59	60–64
Good	33	40	36	23	8
Average	48	47	47	50	59
Poor	19	13	17	27	33
Total ($N=1217$)	100	100	100	100	100

Chi-square = 43.916, df = 6, $p = 0.000$ sig.

Table 5.7 Prospects of skills upgrading or professional development over the next 5 years by ethnicity (per cent)

Perceived upgrading prospects	Ethnicity			
	Chinese	Malay	Indian	Others
Good	30	43	37	44
Average	50	41	45	44
Poor	20	15	18	13
Total ($N=1216$)	100	100	100	100

Chi-square = 13.165, df = 6, $p = 0.040$ sig.

Table 5.8 Prospects of skills upgrading or professional development over the next 5 years by occupational status (per cent)

Perceived upgrading prospects	Survey 2001	Occupational status		
		Service	Intermediate	Working
Good	33	46	32	13
Average	48	45	52	48
Poor	19	10	16	39
Total ($N=1215$)	100	100	100	100

Chi-square = 160.987, df = 4, $p = 0.000$ sig.

Table 5.9 Prospects of skills upgrading or professional development over the next 5 years by class (per cent)

Perceived upgrading prospects	Class			
	Upper	Middle	Working	Lower
Good	45	44	27	8
Average	45	45	51	32
Poor	10	10	22	60
Total ($N = 1217$)	100	100	100	100

Chi-square = 114.221, df = 6, $p = 0.000$ sig.

Table 5.10 Currently enrolled in upgrading courses by age (per cent)

Currently enrolled in upgrading course	Survey 2001	Age category (years)			
		15–29	30–44	45–59	60–64
Yes	12	27	8	3	2
No	88	73	93	97	98
Total ($N = 2248$)	100	100	100	100	100

Chi-square = 210.385, df = 3, $p = 0.000$ sig.

Table 5.11 Currently enrolled in upgrading courses by ethnicity (per cent)

Currently enrolled in upgrading course	Ethnicity			
	Chinese	Malay	Indian	Others
Yes	12	11	15	11
No	89	89	85	89
Total ($N = 2248$)	100	100	100	100

Chi-square = 1.797, df = 3, $p = 0.616$ ns.

Career strategies

A pattern similar to those reported above can be discerned in regard to enrolment or planning to enroll in skills upgrading or professional development courses. By and large, young Singaporeans and those in higher status jobs are more likely to be either currently enrolled (Tables 5.10–5.13) or planning to enroll in upgrading courses

Table 5.12 Currently enrolled in upgrading courses by occupational status (per cent)

Currently enrolled in upgrading course	Survey 2001	Occupational status		
		Service	Intermediate	Working
Yes	9	12	9	4
No	91	88	91	96
Total (N = 1456)	100	100	100	100

Chi-square = 22.397, df = 2, p = 0.000 sig.

Table 5.13 Currently enrolled in upgrading courses by class (per cent)

Currently enrolled in upgrading course	Class			
	Upper	Middle	Working	Lower
Yes	14	15	10	5
No	86	85	90	95
Total (N = 2248)	100	100	100	100

Chi-square = 16.109, df = 3, p = 0.001 sig.

Table 5.14 Planning to enroll in upgrading courses by age (per cent)

Planning to enroll in upgrading course	Survey 2001	Age category (years)			
		15–29	30–44	45–59	60–64
Yes	20	41	18	8	1
No	80	59	82	92	99
Total (N = 1982)	100	100	100	100	100

Chi-square = 215.278, df = 3, p = 0.000 sig.

(Tables 5.14–5.17). What may be inferred from these tables is that those "doing well" in their careers are also the ones more likely to pursue skills upgrading or professional development. The issue here is whether this reflects a lack of motivation, a lack of perceived ability, or a lack of opportunity on the part of working class and older Singaporeans. I suspect that it can be attributed to a combination of all three factors. However, given that more training courses at subsidized rates are being made available to workers, there is a good chance that we will see an increase in the proportion of workers with low education pursuing skills upgrading.

Table 5.15 Planning to enroll in upgrading courses by ethnicity (per cent)

Currently enrolled in upgrading course	Ethnicity			
	Chinese	Malay	Indian	Others
Yes	19	23	22	20
No	81	77	79	80
Total (N= 1982)	100	100	100	100

Chi-square = 2.598, df = 3, p = 0.458 ns.

Table 5.16 Planning to enroll in upgrading courses by occupational status (per cent)

Planning to enroll in upgrading course	Survey 2001	Occupational status		
		Service	Intermediate	Working
Yes	21	31	16	9
No	79	69	84	91
Total (N= 1324)	100	100	100	100

Chi-square = 74.868, df = 2, p = 0.000 sig.

Table 5.17 Planning to enroll in upgrading courses by class (per cent)

Currently enrolled in upgrading course	Class			
	Upper	Middle	Working	Lower
Yes	36	18	20	18
No	64	82	80	82
Total (N= 1217)	100	100	100	100

Chi-square = 7.609, df = 3, p = 0.055 borderline sig.

Social mobility

From work-related processes, we move on to the broader process of social mobility. Table 5.18 compares the occupational status profile of respondents with that of the respondents' fathers.[4] It shows that

---

[4] It should be noted that, due to some limitations in the dataset, we were unable to use sophisticated analysis techniques in the mobility tables reported in this section. Hence, the findings presented in this section should be considered indicative, rather than definitive.

52 per cent of the respondents, as compared to 46 per cent of the respondents' fathers are in service class occupations; and 27 per cent, as compared to 18 per cent of the respondents' fathers, are in intermediate class occupations. The proportion of respondents in working class occupations is 22 per cent, much lower than the 35 per cent for the respondents' fathers. This provides some indication of the extent of inter-generational upward social mobility.

Unlike Table 5.18, which compares the occupational status profiles of respondents and respondents' fathers, Table 5.19 looks at the relationship between the respondent's occupational status and that of his or her father's occupational status. Table 5.19 shows that there is a high degree of class reproduction and upward social mobility across one generation. For instance, 61 per cent of respondents' fathers in service class occupations have children who are also in service class occupations; while 48 per cent of respondents' fathers in intermediate class occupations have children moving into service class occupations. However, there is some degree of downward

Table 5.18 Social mobility: respondent (R)'s occupational status and R's father's occupational status (per cent)

Occupational status	R's father's	R's
Service	46	52
Intermediate	18	27
Working	35	22
Total ($N=947$)	100	100

Table 5.19 Social mobility: respondent (R)'s occupational status by R's father's occupational status (per cent)

R's occupational status	R's Father's occupational status		
	Service	Intermediate	Working
Service	61	48	41
Intermediate	25	32	26
Working	14	20	33
Total (N = 947)	100	100	100

Chi-square = 50.947, df = 4, $p=0.000$ sig.

mobility as well, such as the 14 per cent in working class occupations who originated from service class backgrounds. Our data suggest that many of the "downwardly mobile" are young and, as Chiew (1991:211–212) puts it, "have not yet attained their highest status in their career cycles."

Table 5.20 suggests that the three major ethnic categories in Singapore—Chinese, Malays, and Indians—have experienced some degree of upward inter-generational mobility. The extent of upward social mobility, relative to that of respondents' father's occupational status, is proportionally higher for the minority Malays and Indians. For instance, our comparison of respondents and respondents' fathers' occupational status indicates that the proportion of Malays in service class occupations climbed from 23 to 37 per cent across one generation, while that for the Chinese rose only 3 per cent—from 51 to 54 per cent.

Table 5.21 shows that the bulk of Singaporeans, comprising predominantly those in the middle class and the working class, have experienced some degree of upward intergenerational mobility. The middle class saw the proportion of those in service class occupations rising from 54 to 64 per cent across one generation. Among the self-identified lower class, the proportion in working class occupations rose from 42 to 63 per cent, while that in service class occupations declined from 42 to 17 per cent, an evidence of downward mobility.

Table 5.20 Social mobility: respondent (R)'s occupational status by R's father's occupational status by ethnicity (per cent)

Occupational status	Ethnicity					
	Chinese (*N* = 744)		**Malay** (*N* = 124)		**Indian** (*N* = 67)	
	R's father	R's	R's father	R's	R's father	R's
Service	51	54	23	37	37	49
Intermediate	14	25	34	31	37	36
Working	35	21	44	32	25	15
Total (*N* = 935)	100	100	100	100	100	100

Chinese sub-sample: Chi-square = 36.516, df = 4, p = 0.000 sig.
Malay sub-sample: Chi-square = 13.559, df = 4, p = 0.009 sig.
Indian sub-sample: Chi-square = 2.582, df = 4, p = 0.630 ns.

Table 5.21 Social mobility: respondent (R)'s occupational status by R's father's occupational status by class (per cent)

Occupational status	Class							
	Upper (N = 18)		Middle (N = 390)		Working (N = 496)		Lower (N = 41)	
	R's father	R's	R's father	R's	R's father	R's	R's father	R's
Service	61	67	54	64	41	45	42	17
Intermediate	11	28	14	25	22	28	17	20
Working	28	6	32	11	38	27	42	63
Total (N = 945)	100	100	100	100	100	100	100	100

Upper class sub-sample: Chi-square = 2.302, df = 4, $p = 0.680$ ns.
Middle class sub-sample: Chi-square = 38.973, df = 4, $p = 0.000$ sig.
Working class sub-sample: Chi-square = 13.599, df = 4, $p = 0.009$ sig.
Lower class sub-sample: Chi-square = 13.537, df = 4, $p = 0.009$ sig.

However, since the self-identified lower class constitutes only 4.3 per cent of those in employment, the extent of downward mobility reported here is probably not a cause for concern.

Another class dynamics examined in this study relates to perceived changes in financial situation. Table 5.22 shows that the proportion of Singaporeans describing their current financial situation as either "above average" or "well-off" is 17 per cent, whereas the proportion describing their past financial situation in similar terms is 9 per cent. It can also be observed that close to three-fourths (73 per cent) of Singaporeans placed themselves in the "average" category, which does give the appearance of a movement towards a more homogeneous class distribution in Singapore. Across the different ethnic categories, the proportions of Singaporeans who described themselves as "poor" have declined between the time when they were about 15 years of age and the time of the survey. This suggests that Singaporeans generally experienced an improvement in their financial situation.

In regard to the impact of self-identified class on perception of past and current financial situation, it could again be observed that there is a wide gap between the lower class and the higher classes (Table 5.23). Close to half of lower class Singaporeans described themselves as poor both in the "past" and at "present". Interestingly,

Table 5.22 Perceived current financial situation by perceived financial situation when R was about 15 years old by ethnicity (per cent)

Perceived financial situation	Survey 2001		Ethnicity					
			Chinese (N = 1737)		Malay (N = 307)		Indian (N = 173)	
	Past	Current	Past	Current	Past	Current	Past	Current
Well-off	1	1	1	1	1	0	1	1
Above average	8	16	8	17	8	13	10	17
Average	65	73	64	73	73	76	64	70
Poor	26	10	27	10	19	10	25	12
Total (N = 2217)	100	100	100	100	100	100	100	100

Overall sample: Chi-square = 117.893, df = 9, p = 0.000 sig.
Chinese sub-sample: Chi-square = 249.735, df = 9, p = 0.000 sig.
Malay sub-sample: Chi-square = 29.975, df = 9, p = 0.000 sig.
Indian sub-sample: Chi-square = 108.828, df = 9, p = 0.000 sig.

Table 5.23 Perceived current financial situation by perceived financial situation when R was about 15 years old by class (per cent)

Financial situation	Class							
	Upper (N = 43)		Middle (N = 926)		Working (N = 1147)		Lower (N = 131)	
	Past	Current	Past	Current	Past	Current	Past	Current
Well-off	0	2	1	1	1	0	0	0
Above average	9	21	12	23	7	12	2	1
Average	70	65	68	71	65	78	49	52
Poor	20	12	19	5	28	10	49	47
Total (N= 2247)	100	100	100	100	100	100	100	100

Upper class sub-sample: Chi-square = 24.420, df = 6, $p = 0.000$ sig.
Middle class sub-sample: Chi-square = 117.893, df = 9, $p = 0.000$ sig.
Working class sub-sample: Chi-square = 155.253, df = 9, $p = 0.000$ sig.
Lower class sub-sample: Chi-square = 12.138, df = 4, $p = 0.016$ sig.

there is a higher proportion of the upper class (12 per cent) describing themselves as "poor", as compared to 5 per cent for the middle class and 10 per cent for the working class. This seems to indicate that the perceived "poverty line" from the perspective of the upper class is much higher than that of the middle class or working class.

6

Problem Areas: Digital Divide and Sandwich Generation

This chapter focuses on two problem areas: digital divide and sandwich generation. The former relates to work skills, while the latter pertains to financial needs. As in previous chapters, the analyses will be conducted in terms of age, ethnicity, and class.

Digital divide

In recent years, one of the key concerns in a Singapore undergoing economic restructuring is that of the digital divide, or the gap separating the computer literate from the computer illiterate.

Our findings on this topic resemble those relating to "propensity for enrolling in upgrading courses" reported in Chapter 5. Tables 6.1–6.9 present the results on the digital divide. Apart from suggesting that the digital divide may not be an ethnic phenomenon (Tables 6.2 and 6.6), our data reveal that older Singaporeans (Table 6.1) and those in working class occupations (Table 6.3) and the lower class (Table 6.4) are more likely to be found on the wrong side of the digital divide. Paradoxically, these same categories of Singaporeans are also less likely to indicate "perceived

Table 6.1 "I am quite comfortable with using the computer" by age (per cent)

Feel comfortable using the computer	Survey 2001	Age category (years)			
		15–29	30–44	45–59	60–64
High	67	87	67	47	25
Medium	5	5	4	6	3
Low	28	8	28	47	72
Total (N = 2032)	100	100	100	100	100

Chi-square = 310.909, df = 6, p = 0.000 sig.

Table 6.2 "I am quite comfortable with using the computer" by ethnicity (per cent)

Feel comfortable using the computer	Survey 2001	Ethnicity			
		Chinese	Malay	Indian	Others
High	67	67	63	72	69
Medium	5	4	5	7	4
Low	28	29	32	22	27
Total (N = 2033)	100	100	100	100	100

Chi-square = 7.681, df = 6, p = 0.262 sig.

Table 6.3 "I am quite comfortable with using the computer" by class (per cent)

Feel comfortable using the computer	Survey 2001	Class			
		Upper	Middle	Working	Lower
High	67	87	77	61	31
Medium	5	3	4	6	7
Low	28	10	19	33	62
Total (N = 2034)	100	100	100	100	100

Chi-square = 131.402, df = 6, p = 0.000 sig.

Table 6.4 "I am quite comfortable with using the computer" by occupational status (per cent)

Feel comfortable using the computer	Survey 2001	Occupational status		
		Service	Intermediate	Working
High	69	83	75	31
Medium	4	2	4	7
Low	28	15	21	62
Total ($N=1324$)	100	100	100	100

Chi-square = 284.550, df = 4, p = 0.000 sig.

Table 6.5 "My lack of ability in using the computer will hinder my finding a job or hinder my career advancement" by age (per cent)

Perceived inadequacy	Survey 2001	Age category (years)			
		15–29	30–44	45–59	60–64
High	71	85	69	61	44
Medium	5	4	4	6	4
Low	25	11	27	33	51
Total ($N=2018$)	100	100	100	100	100

Chi-square = 126.220, df = 6, p = 0.000 sig.

Table 6.6 "My lack of ability in using the computer will hinder my finding a job or hinder my career advancement" by ethnicity (per cent)

Perceived inadequacy	Survey 2001	Ethnicity			
		Chinese	Malay	Indian	Others
High	71	69	78	73	73
Medium	5	5	3	6	4
Low	25	26	19	21	23
Total ($N=2017$)	100	100	100	100	100

Chi-square = 11.355, df = 6, p = 0.078 ns.

inadequacy of computer skills" (Tables 6.5, 6.7–6.9). A logical explanation is that because older and working class Singaporeans are not in jobs that require computer skills, they are less likely to find it necessary to seek computer skills training.

Table 6.7 "My lack of ability in using the computer will hinder my finding a job or hinder my career advancement" by class (per cent)

Perceived inadequacy	Survey 2001	Class			
		Upper	Middle	Working	Lower
High	71	64	70	72	61
Medium	5	3	5	4	4
Low	25	33	25	24	35
Total ($N = 2017$)	100	100	100	100	100

Chi-square = 9.579, df = 6, $p = 0.144$ ns.

Table 6.8 "My lack of ability in using the computer will hinder my finding a job or hinder my career advancement" by occupational status (per cent)

Perceived inadequacy	Survey 2001	Occupational Status		
		Service	Intermediate	Working
High	70	73	74	61
Medium	5	3	6	6
Low	25	24	20	33
Total ($N = 1345$)	100	100	100	100

Chi-square = 24.947, df = 4, $p = 0.000$ sig.

Table 6.9 "My lack of ability in using the computer will hinder my finding a job or hinder my career advancement" by "I am quite comfortable using the computer" (per cent)

Perceived inadequacy	Feel comfortable using the computer		
	High	Medium	Low
High	79	45	52
Medium	3	44	2
Low	18	12	46
Total ($N = 1883$)	100	100	100

Chi-square = 475.384, df = 4, $p = 0.000$ sig.

Sandwich generation

Besides the digital divide issue, another problem affecting people in advanced industrial societies is that relating to the "sandwich" generation. This problem has its roots in the following demographic or social phenomena: the greying population, longer life expectancy, lengthening dependency period, growing demand for higher education, and the fact that older age cohorts possess lower educational qualifications and were less inclined to practise financial planning for their twilight years. In this study, a person is deemed to be in the "sandwich" generation if he or she indicates a high degree of difficulty in providing financial support for his or her parents as well as children (see items 3E-14 and 3E-15 of the questionnaire).

Table 6.10 shows that those in the middle age category — aged 45–59 — are more likely to be "sandwiched". However, while Table 6.11 displays the same result, the indication here is that "sandwich" is not an age phenomenon, nor is it an ethnic phenomenon

Table 6.10 "Sandwich" by age (per cent)

Extent of "sandwich"	Survey 2001	Age category (years)			
		15–29	30–44	45–59	60–64
High	25	18	23	30	28
Medium	19	36	20	15	10
Low	56	46	57	55	62
Total (N = 1288)	100	100	100	100	100

Chi-square = 33.798, df = 6, $p = 0.000$ sig.

Table 6.11 "Sandwich" score by age (high score = 3)

Age (years)	"Sandwich" score
15–29	1.72
30–44	1.66
45–59	1.75
60–64	1.66
N = 1287	1.70
	Ns

(Tables 6.12 and 6.13). Not unexpectedly, it is a class phenomenon: the people in the lower class category or working class occupations are more likely to experience being "sandwiched" (Tables 6.14–6.17).

Table 6.12 "Sandwich" by ethnicity (per cent)

Extent of "sandwich"	Survey 2001	Ethnicity			
		Chinese	Malay	Indian	Others
High	25	25	30	25	24
Medium	19	20	16	15	18
Low	56	56	54	61	59
Total ($N=1288$)	100	100	100	100	100

Chi-square = 5.297, df = 6, $p = 0.506$ ns.

Table 6.13 "Sandwich" score by ethnicity (high score = 3)

Ethnicity	"Sandwich" score
Chinese	1.69
Malay	1.77
Indian	1.63
Others	1.65
$N=1287$	1.70
	Ns

Table 6.14 "Sandwich" by class (per cent)

Extent of "Sandwich"	Survey 2001	Class			
		Upper	Middle	Working	Lower
High	25	39	17	27	76
Medium	19	4	19	20	13
Low	56	57	64	54	11
Total ($N=1286$)	100	100	100	100	100

Chi-square = 111.545, df = 6, $p = 0.000$ sig.

Table 6.15 "sandwich" score by class (high score = 3)

Class	"Sandwich" score
Upper	1.79
Middle	1.53
Working	1.73
Lower	2.64
N = 1287	1.70
	Sig.

Table 6.16 "Sandwich" by occupational status (per cent)

Extent of "Sandwich"	Survey 2001	Occupational status		
		Service	Intermediate	Working
High	22	13	24	39
Medium	19	18	22	18
Low	59	69	54	43
Total (N = 966)	100	100	100	100

Chi-square = 72.589, df = 4, $p = 0.000$ sig.

Table 6.17 "Sandwich" score by occupational status (high score = 3)

Occupational status	"Sandwich" score
Service	1.44
Intermediate	1.69
Working	1.96
N = 965	1.64
	Sig.

7

One-to-two-Roomers, Three-Roomers, and Citizen Population Compared

The previous chapters dealt with the main sample, and thereby the general population. This chapter was originally intended to compare the one-to-three-roomers with the general population. The one-to-three roomers were singled out for comparisons as they are often thought of as "low income" Singaporeans.

However, our initial exploration of the survey data revealed that, on most items, the one-to-three roomers as a category, not unexpectedly, exhibit characteristics usually associated with people possessing low economic means, but, in regard to subjective well-being, they are quite similar to the general population. On this basis, there may be a case to argue that the one-to-three roomers are not very different from the general population, but the data also suggest the need to analyse the one-to-two-roomers separately from the three-roomers.

Indeed, a recent Housing and Development Board (HDB) (2000:83) report indicates that one-to-two-roomers are qualitatively different from the three-roomers in terms of ownership or non-ownership of the property they occupy. For instance, the proportions of one- and two-roomers who do not own the HDB apartment they live in are 88.4 and 75.0 per cent, respectively, whereas the comparative figure for the three-roomers is only 2.3 per cent.

The next section will compare the profiles of the one-to-two-roomers and three-roomers with that of the general population. Following which, we will compare the social orientations of the three categories. The final section will compare their utilization and evaluation of a list of twelve types of social services.

Profiles compared

Tables 7.1–7.5 compare the demographic profiles of the one-to-two-roomers with that of the three-roomers and general population. It can be seen that close to half of the one-to-two-roomers are aged above 45 years (Table 7.2). The Chinese are over-represented among the three-roomers, whereas the minorities, especially the Malays, are over-represented among the one-to-two-roomers (Table 7.3). In

Table 7.1 Housing Type (per cent)

Housing type	Population (N = 2248)	one to three roomers (N = 497)
Landed property	5	0
Private apartment	3	0
HDB five-room and executive	26	0
four-room	39	0
Three-room	24	83
One-and two-room	3	17
Total	100	100

Table 7.2 Age composition (per cent)

Age category (years)	Population (N = 2250)	Three-roomers (N = 413)	One-to-two-roomers (N = 84)
15–29	30	17	19
30–44	38	39	33
45–59	27	31	29
60–64	5	13	19
Total	100	100	100

terms of monthly household income, while the proportion of the general population with less than $1000 monthly household income is 8 per cent, that for the one-to-two-roomers is 45 per cent (Table 7.4). Of the 59 per cent of the one-to-two-roomers who are in paid employment, close to two-thirds are in working class jobs, compared to about a one-third in the case of three-roomers (Table 7.5). The one-to-two-roomers are, not unexpectedly, more likely to place themselves in the "lower class" of both the six- and four-class

Table 7.3 Ethnic composition (per cent)

Ethnicity	Population (N = 2250)	Three-roomers (N = 416)	One-to-two-roomers (N = 84)
Chinese	77	82	67
Malay	14	11	23
Indian	8	6	10
Others	1	1	1
Total	100	100	100

Table 7.4 Monthly household income (per cent)

Income category	Population (N = 2250)	Three-roomers (N = 393)	One-to-two-roomers (N = 83)
$8000 and over	7	3	0
$3000–7999	41	31	10
$1000–2999	40	51	46
Below $1000	8	14	45
Refused/DK	4	0	0
Total	100	100	100

Table 7.5 Occupational status (per cent)

Occupational status	Population (N = 1456)	Three-roomers (N = 248)	One-to-two-roomers (N = 49)
Service class	48	36	18
Intermediate class	26	29	22
Working class	26	36	59
Total	100	100	100

Table 7.6 Subjective class structure (per cent)

Six-category class ladder	Population	Three-roomers	One-to-two-roomers	One-to-two-roomers	Three-roomers	Population	Four-category class ladder
Upper	1	1	1	0	1	2	Upper
Upper Middle	6) 87	2) 74	6) 62				
Middle Middle	49)	37)	27)	29	28	42	Middle
Lower Middle	32)	35)	29)				
Upper Lower	9	16	21	49	57	51	Working
Lower Lower	3	9	16	23	13	6	Lower
Total	100	100	100	100	100	100	Total

structures (Table 7.6) as well as the "poor" category of the item "perceived financial situation" (Table 7.7). They also tend to be less optimistic about their "financial situation over the next 5 years" (Table 7.8). Interestingly, they are more likely to report a budget surplus than even the general population (Table 7.9). It looks like they are likely to be quite successful at spending within their means, probably supplemented by some financial help from outside the household.

Table 7.7 Perceived financial situation (per cent)

Perceived financial situation	Population	Three-roomers	One-to-two-roomers
Well-off	1	1	1
Better than average	16	9	12
Average	73	77	64
Poor	10	14	23
Total	100	100	100

Table 7.8 Optimism: Perceived financial situation over the next 5 years (per cent)

Perceived financial situation	Population	Three-roomers	One-to-two-roomers
Better than now	33	27	27
About the same as now	58	61	57
Worse than now	10	12	16
Total	100	100	100

Table 7.9 Household budget situation (per cent)

Household budget situation	Population	Three-roomers	One-to-two-roomers
Income more than expenditure	29	27	35
Income = expenditure	53	53	48
Income less than expenditure	17	20	18
Total	100	100	100

Social orientations compared

Table 7.10 indicates that, in relative terms, the one-to-two roomers are somewhat more likely to give "hard work" and "luck" a high ranking as success factors. They are therefore rather similar to the "lower class" reported in Chapter 4. Our explanation for this finding is that even as the lower class think of "hard work" as giving them hope for upward mobility, their seeing "luck" as a success factor makes it easier for them to accept their lack of success.

Nevertheless, the one-to-two-roomers are, as compared to the three-roomers, somewhat more likely to think of Singapore as a "land of opportunity for everyone" (Table 7.11), and "a good place to raise one's children" (Table 7.12), but they are also more likely to agree that "the government should give financial assistance to the poor" (Table 7.13) and "Singapore unions ensure that their members are treated fairly" (Tables 7.15). What may be inferred from these findings is that, while the latter two orientations reflect differences in the

Table 7.10 Success factors (mean score), where 1 = most important

Attribute	Population	Three-roomers	One-to-two-roomers
Ability	2.60	2.72	2.89
Education	1.83	1.92	2.06
Hard work	2.53	2.49	2.31
Connection	3.71	3.77	3.79
Luck	4.33	4.10	3.95

Table 7.11 "Everyone in Singapore has a good chance to achieve a high standard of living" (per cent)

"Everyone in Singapore has a good chance to achieve a high standard of living"	Population	Three-roomers	One-to-two-roomers
Agree	78	74	79
Neutral	4	5	0
Disagree	18	20	22
Total	100	100	100

Table 7.12 "Singapore is a good place to raise one's children" (per cent)

"Singapore is a good place to raise one's children"	Population	Three-roomers	One-to-two-roomers
Agree	78	75	79
Neutral	7	7	6
Disagree	15	18	14
Total	100	100	100

Table 7.13 "The government should give financial assistance to the poor" (per cent)

"The government should give financial assistance to the poor"	Population	Three-roomers	One-to-two-roomers
Agree	95	95	99
Neutral	3	2	0
Disagree	2	3	1
Total	100	100	100

Table 7.14 "People who are more successful have a responsibility to help the less successful ones" (per cent)

"People who are more successful have a responsibility to help the less successful ones"	Population	Three-roomers	One-to-two-roomers
Agree	87	85	80
Neutral	5	9	1
Disagree	8	7	19
Total	100	100	100

Table 7.15 "Singapore unions ensure that their members are treated fairly" (per cent)

"Singapore unions ensure that their members are treated fairly"	Population	Three-roomers	One-to-two-roomers
Agree	64	65	75
Neutral	19	19	9
Disagree	17	17	16
Total	100	100	100

possession of economic means, the former two orientations, together with the finding on ranking of success factors (Table 7.10), indicate some convergence in social orientations among Singaporeans.

However, there are some interesting, but seemingly paradoxical, findings as well. Table 7.14 indicates that proportionally more of the one-to-two-roomers believe in self-reliance: 19 per cent of one-to-two-roomers, as compared to 8 per cent of the general population, do not agree with the statement that "people who are more successful have a responsibility to help the less successful ones". The one-to-two-roomers are also more likely to report a high propensity for political participation, moderately low perceived participation opportunity, and therefore somewhat high political alienation (Tables 7.16–7.18). This overlaps with our earlier finding that the

Table 7.16 Participation propensity (per cent)

Participation propensity	Population	Three-roomers	One-to-two-roomers
High	13	10	17
Medium	56	43	44
Low	32	47	39
Total	100	100	100

Table 7.17 Perceived participation opportunity (per cent)

Perceived participation opportunity	Population	Three-roomers	One-to-two-roomers
High	8	10	13
Medium	45	32	20
Low	47	58	67
Total	100	100	100

Table 7.18 Political alienation score (per cent)

Political alienation score	Population	Three-roomers	One-to-two-roomers
High	23	18	33
Medium	73	74	62
Low	4	9	5
Total	100	100	100

working class and lower class are more likely to score "positive" on political alienation (cf. Chapter 4). Another seemingly paradoxical finding is that the one-to-two-roomers are, in relative terms, more likely to report that they have "close friends of a different race" (Table 7.19). This probably corresponds to that fact that the minorities, who are more likely than the Chinese to report having cross-ethnic ties, are over-represented in the one-to-two-roomers category.

On most of the other items (Tables 7.20–7.33), the one-to-two-roomers are, not unexpectedly, likely to manifest characteristics that reflect their possessing less economic means than the general population. Specifically, in relative terms, one-to-two-roomers

Table 7.19 "Have close friends of a different race" (per cent)

"Have close friends of a different race"	Population	Three-roomers	One-to-two-roomers
Agree	75	69	79
Neutral	4	5	1
Disagree	21	26	20
Total	100	100	100

Table 7.20 "Successful people in Singapore tend to look down on the less successful ones" (per cent)

"Successful people in Singapore tend to look down on the less successful ones"	Population	Three-roomers	One-to-two-roomers
Agree	47	53	54
Neutral	10	11	5
Disagree	43	37	42
Total	100	100	100

Table 7.21 "I am proud to be a Singaporean" (per cent)

"I am proud to be a Singaporean"	Population	Three-roomers	One-to-two-roomers
Agree	94	90	86
Neutral	3	3	4
Disagree	3	7	11
Total	100	100	100

Table 7.22 "Singapore has more good points than bad points" (per cent)

"Singapore has more good points than bad points"	Population	Three-roomers	One-to-two-roomers
Agree	85	85	80
Neutral	10	9	1
Disagree	5	7	19
Total	100	100	100

Table 7.23 "Singapore is a good place to make a living" (per cent)

"Singapore is a good place to make a living"	Population	Three-roomers	One-to-two-roomers
Agree	69	61	55
Neutral	8	7	2
Disagree	23	32	42
Total	100	100	100

Table 7.24 Perceived business prospects over the next 5 years (per cent)

Perceived business prospects	Population	Three-roomers	One-to-two-roomers
Very good	2	4	0
Good	11	4	0
Average	60	75	100
Poor	22	8	0
Very poor	1	4	0
NA	4	5	0
Total	100	100	100

Table 7.25 Perceived career prospects over the next 5 years (per cent)

Perceived career prospects	Population	Three-roomers	One-to-two-roomers
Good	32	23	21
Average	48	57	60
Poor	20	19	19
Total	100	100	100

Table 7.26 Prospects of skills upgrading or professional development over the next 5 years (per cent)

Perceived upgrading prospects	Population	Three-roomers	One-to-two-roomers
Good	33	29	26
Average	48	45	49
Poor	19	26	26
Total	100	100	100

Table 7.27 Currently enrolled in upgrading courses (per cent)

Currently enrolled in upgrading courses	Population	Three-roomers	One-to-two-roomers
Yes	12	7	6
No	88	93	94
Total	100	100	100

Table 7.28 Planning to enrol in upgrading courses (per cent)

Planning to enroll in upgrading courses	Population	Three-roomers	One-to-two-roomers
Yes	20	10	9
No	80	90	91
Total	100	100	100

Table 7.29 "Feel comfortable using the computer" (per cent)

"Feel comfortable using the computer"	Population	Three-roomers	One-to-two-roomers
High	67	47	39
Medium	5	5	8
Low	28	37	44
Total	100	100	100

Table 7.30 "Perceived inadequacy of computer skills" (per cent)

Perceived inadequacy	Population	Three-roomers	One-to-two-roomers
High	71	59	56
Medium	5	6	7
Low	25	27	35
Total	100	100	100

Table 7.31 Household receiving outside help (per cent)

Household receiving outside help	Population	Three-roomers	One-to-two-roomers
Yes	4	9	16
No	96	91	85
Total	100	100	100

Table 7.32 Sources of help among those receiving outside help (per cent)

Sources of help	Population ($N = 98$)	Three-roomers ($N = 38$)	One-to-two-roomers ($N = 13$)
Friends or relatives	61	89	69
Charities	23	5	0
Combination	16	5	31
Total	100	100	100

Table 7.33 Overall life satisfaction (per cent)

Overall life satisfaction	Population	Three-roomers	One-to-two-roomers
Very satisfied	10	5	4
Satisfied	76	77	70
Not satisfied	13	16	19
Not satisfied at all	1	2	7
Total	100	100	100

are (a) more likely to believe that "successful people look down on the less successful ones"; (b) less likely to indicate that they are "proud to be a Singaporean"; (c) less likely to think that "Singapore has more good points than bad points"; (d) less likely to consider Singapore as a "good place to make a living"; (e) more likely to rate their business and career prospects as "average"; (f) less optimistic about future skills upgrading; (g) less likely to be involved in or planning to enrol in skills upgrading courses; (h) less likely to feel "comfortable with using the computer", but also less likely to perceive inadequacy in computer skills; (i) more likely to be receiving financial help from outside the household; (j) more likely to use a combination of sources of financial help — friends, relatives, and

Table 7.34 Extent of "sandwich" (per cent)

Extent of "sandwich"	Population	Three-roomers	One-to-two-roomers
High	25	41	24
Medium	19	18	19
Low	56	41	57
Total	100	100	100

charitable organisations — from outside the household; and (k) less likely to report overall life satisfaction.

Unlike the one-to-two-roomers, who constitute the focal category in the above analysis, the three-roomers tend to occupy an intermediate position between the general population and the one-to-two-roomers. There is, however, one important exception. Table 7.34 indicates that the three-roomers are more likely to be affected by the "sandwich" generation problem. This probably stems from the fact that the "three-roomers" category contains a higher proportion of middle aged people.

Utilization and evaluation of social services or programmes compared

In Table 7.35, one observes that the proportions of people who mentioned that they require the social services listed in the questionnaire are quite low, below 5 per cent for each social service type. However, it should be pointed out that in a citizen population of close to 3 million people, 5 per cent is equivalent to about 150,000 actual or potential service users in absolute terms.

Table 7.35 also indicates that, compared to the three-roomers and the general population, the one-to-two-roomers are more likely to report that they require the services of the social agencies or programmes in the list. In relative terms, they are less likely to mention that they need the services of vocational assessment programmes, student care centres, or child care centres. Instead, they are more likely to mention services like home shelters for the aged and seniors activity centres. This is hardly surprising, given that the

Table 7.35 Social agencies or programmes from which help is required (per cent)

Social agencies/programmes	Population (*N* = 2248)	Three-roomers (*N* = 413)	One-to-two-roomers (*N* = 84)
1. Crisis shelters	1.2	0.5	1.2
2. Home shelters for the aged	1.5	1.7	3.6
3. Homes for the disabled	0.6	0.5	4.8
4. Vocational assessment programmes	1.5	1.5	1.2
5. Day activity centres for the disabled	0.5	0.2	2.4
6. Counselling centres (for domestic violence and abuse)	0.4	1.0	2.4
7. Family service centres	1.0	1.2	2.4
8. Student care centres	2.2	1.5	1.2
9. Child care centres	3.7	3.4	2.4
10. Seniors activity centres	2.3	3.6	4.8
11. Social day centres for the aged	1.1	1.7	2.4
12. Befriender service (volunteer programme for the lonely elderly)	1.1	0.2	2.4
13. Mentioned one or more social agencies or programmes	10.3	12.3	14.3

one-to-two-roomers category contains a higher proportion of older people than either the three-roomers or the general population category.

In regard to actual utilization of the social services, Table 7.36 shows that while the general population and the three-roomers used a wider range of services, the one-to-two-roomers utilized only two services from the list: homes for the disabled and seniors activity centres. It seems that the three-roomers are somewhat more likely

Table 7.36 Social agencies or programmes utilized (per cent)

Social agencies/ programmes	Population (N = 2248)	Three-roomers (N = 413)	One-to-two-roomers (N = 84)
1. Crisis shelters	0	0	0
2. Home shelters for the aged	0.6	0.7	0
3. Homes for the disabled	0.1	0	2.4
4. Vocational assessment programme	0.1	0	0
5. Day activity centres for the disabled	0.1	0	0
6. Counselling centres (for domestic violence and abuse)	0.1	0.5	0
7. Family service centres	0.1	0.5	0
8. Student care centres	0.7	0.2	0
9. Child care centres	2.0	2.2	0
10. Seniors activity centres	0.9	1.7	1.2
11. Social day centres for the aged	0.1	0.5	0
12. Befriender service (volunteer programme for the lonely elderly)	0.1	0	0

to utilize counselling centres (for domestic violence and abuse) and family service centres. This is perhaps an indication that three-roomers are, in relative terms, more likely to encounter relationship problems within their families. The relationship problems may in turn stem from the fact that a higher proportion of the three-roomers are found in the "sandwich" generation (cf. Table 7.34).

Apart from a filter question designed to gauge the extent of utilization of the social services listed, this study asked the respondents to evaluate the social services along the dimensions of "convenience" and "affordability". Table 7.37 shows that, in relative terms, the one-to-two-roomers rated fewer of the social services as "convenient".[5]

---

[5] For this analysis, a social service is deemed to be "convenient" if it is thought to be so by more than 50 per cent of those who mentioned that they require the particular social service. The same yardstick is used for measuring "affordability".

Table 7.37 Evaluation of social agencies or programmes: Those who rated the service as convenient as a proportion of those who mentioned they need the service

Social agencies/ programmes	Population	Three-roomers	One-to-two-roomers
1. Crisis shelters	12/26	1/1	1/2
2. Home shelters for the aged	23/33	3/3	3/7
3. Homes for the disabled	8/13	4/4	0/2
4. Vocational assessment programme	17/33	1/1	3/6
5. Day activity centres for the disabled	5/11	2/2	0/1
6. Counselling centres (for domestic violence and abuse)	5/8	2/2	0/4
7. Family service centres	15/22	2/2	3/5
8. Student care centres	36/49	1/1	5/6
9. Child care centres	76/84	2/2	13/14
10. Seniors activity centres	36/51	3/4	11/15
11. Social day centres for the aged	15/26	2/2	3/7
12. Befriender service (volunteer programme for the lonely elderly)	14/25	2/2	0/1

Note: In each cell, the numerator refers to the number of persons who rated that particular service as convenient, while the denominator refers to the number of persons who mentioned that they need that particular service.

However, the seniors activity centres, which heads the list of social services mentioned most frequently by the one-to-two-roomers, was rated as "convenient". In regard to affordability, Table 7.38 indicates that the three-roomers rated only two of the social services as "affordable", compared to four in the case of the one-to-two-roomers.

A general pattern that emerged from a comparison of the one-to-two-roomers and the three-roomers is that while the former are more likely to mention that they need the social services in the list, they are less likely to utilize these services as well as rate them as

Table 7.38 Evaluation of social agencies or programmes: Those who rated the service as affordable as a proportion of those who mentioned they need the service

Social agencies/ programmes	Population	Three-roomers	One-to-two-roomers
1. Crisis shelters	7/26	0/1	0/2
2. Home shelters for the aged	17/33	1/3	6/7
3. Homes for the disabled	6/13	3/4	1/2
4. Vocational assessment programme	15/33	0/1	1/6
5. Day activity centres for the disabled	2/11	1/2	1/1
6. Counselling centres (for domestic violence and abuse)	6/8	1/2	2/4
7. Family service centres	11/22	1/2	3/5
8. Student care centres	33/49	0/1	2/6
9. Child care centres	57/84	0/2	9/14
10. Seniors activity centres	33/51	3/4	8/15
11. Social day centres for the aged	15/26	1/2	4/7
12. Befriender service (volunteer programme for the lonely elderly)	10/25	0/2	1/1

"convenient", but slightly more likely to rate the services as "affordable". At the risk of oversimplifying, it could perhaps be inferred that while the one-to-two-roomers encounter a problem of "inconvenience", the three-roomers face a problem of "unaffordability", in regard to the utilization of the social services they need.

8

Conclusion: Does Class Matter in Singapore?

The overall picture emerging from our analysis is that class (and age) matters more than ethnicity in explaining the social orientations of Singaporeans. This suggests that there are good reasons for social policy in Singapore to pay close attention to the class dimension. The sections below summarize what we have found about class structure and social orientations in Singapore.

Class structure

1. In terms of objective criteria, such as income, occupation, education, and house-type, Singapore has a middle-class majority. However, in terms of subjective class identification, Singapore is almost evenly split between the middle class and the working class.
2. The four-category subjective class scheme provides an effective way to map the class structure in Singapore.

Does class matter?

1. Singaporeans' orientation towards the success factors resonates with that of Singapore's meritocratic values and practices.

Specifically, education, hard work, and ability rank higher than social connection and luck as success factors. By and large, Singaporeans, regardless of class, age, and ethnicity, rank the success factors in the same order. This indicates some convergence or homogeneity in success values.
2. In relative terms, the middle and the working classes, who constitute the vast majority of Singaporeans, are more likely to attribute success to ability and education, while upper and lower class Singaporeans are somewhat more inclined to emphasize "luck" as a success factor.
3. The middle and the working classes are more likely to think of Singapore as a land of opportunity for everyone. Nevertheless, most Singaporeans support the idea of state welfarism and community charity.
4. Singaporeans in working class occupations are more likely to support unionism.
5. With regard to political participation, the middle class have a high participation propensity, but they manifest low political alienation, as they are likely to perceive a smaller or no gap between participation propensity and perceived participation opportunity.
6. The cross-class friendship pattern is a asymmetrical one in the sense that the lower class are less likely to have "higher income" friends, even though all classes claim to have "lower income" friends. Moreover, lower class Singaporeans are more likely to believe that "successful people in Singapore tend to look down on the less successful ones". This finding suggests the potential for, or even the presence of, some degree of class tension.
7. The higher classes are more likely to have cross-ethnic ties.
8. The middle class are somewhat more likely to rate Singapore as "a good place to make a living" and "a good place to raise one's children".
9. The middle class and working class are more likely to express "overall satisfaction" with life.
10. Singaporeans in higher status occupations are more likely to be optimistic about their career prospects and to be enrolled or planning to enroll in skills upgrading or professional development courses.

11. There is a digital divide between those in the service and intermediate class, on one side, and the working class, on the other side. Paradoxically, the latter are less likely to express "perceived inadequacy in computer skills".
12. The "sandwich" generation problem is primarily a class phenomenon. Those in the lower class are more likely to be part of the "sandwich" generation.
13. The one-to-three-roomers are quite similar to the general population in terms of social orientations. However, there is a sharper contrast between the one-to-two-roomers and the general population, with the three-roomers occupying an intermediate position between them. The difference in social orientations can be attributed to class position.
14. With regard to utilization and evaluation of the social services, a general pattern observed is that, as compared to the three-roomers and the general population, the one-to-two-roomers are more likely to mention that they need the social services provided, in particular "homes for the disabled" and "seniors activity centres". The one-to-two-roomers are also less likely to rate the social services they utilize as "convenient", but somewhat more likely to rate them as "affordable".

Does ethnicity matter?

1. By and large, our data show that the minorities generally feel positive towards Singapore.
2. Their orientation towards the success factors are rather similar to the majority Chinese. This indicates some convergence or homogeneity in social orientation towards meritocratic values among Singaporeans, regardless of age, class, and ethnicity. However, the minorities are somewhat more likely to support the view that successful people have a responsibility to help the less successful ones in society.
3. In relative terms, the minorities, especially the Indians, have a higher propensity for political participation. However, because they are just as likely to perceive that there is sufficient

opportunity for participation, they are less likely to feel "political alienated". More generally, political alienation does not appear to be an ethnic phenomenon.
4. The minorities are more likely to have cross-ethnic ties than the Chinese.
5. The minorities have experienced some degree of upward social mobility, and are, in relative terms, more likely to feel optimistic about their future financial situation.
6. With regards to the possible problem areas—digital divide and "sandwich" generation—it seems that class and age matter more than ethnicity.

Does age matter?

1. In relative terms, young Singaporeans (aged 15–29 years) are more likely to think of Singapore as a land of opportunity, but they are somewhat less likely to perceive of Singapore as "a good place to make a living", and less likely to express "overall life satisfaction" than the other age categories.
2. Nevertheless, they are optimistic about their future financial situation and career and skills upgrading prospects. Not surprisingly, they are more likely to "feel comfortable with using the computers", but also more likely to perceive "inadequacy in computer skills".
3. Young Singaporeans score from medium to high on participation propensity, but they are also likely to score high on perceived participation opportunity. Correspondingly, they are less likely to feel "politically alienated", as compared to their middle-age (aged 45–59 years) counterparts.
4. Young Singaporeans are more likely to have "close friends of a different race", while elderly Singaporeans (aged 60–64 years) are the least likely to have cross-ethnic friendship ties.

Appendix I

Six Case Studies[7]

Case study 1

Making ends meet: a low-income family

Profile of Mr R

Age	: 33
Educational level	: Up to Primary 3
Occupation	: Security guard
Household Income	: $850 per month + $200 welfare benefits from Interim (short-term) Financial Assistance Scheme (IFAS)
Type of housing	: Two-room flat
Family	: Wife (aged 30) and two children (son, aged 10, and daughter, aged 7)

---

[7]The preparation of these case studies had benefited from the editorial assistance of Lim Peck Whee.

Everyday life

It was 8:30 pm. Mr R had just returned from work when I met him for the interview. On our way to his two-room apartment, he explained that he reached home late today as something had cropped up at the factory where he worked as a security guard. Nearing his knock off time, the factory manager complained of two men who were harassing his factory workers. The men left only after a police report was made.

As Mr R sat eating his dinner of rice and fried *ikan bilis*, I looked around the house he lived with his wife and two children. The flat is messy and untidy with books, stationery and toys strewn randomly. The floor of the apartment is not covered by plastic mat but left in its original cement flooring. The living room is dominated by a square foldable table which doubles up as a dinner-cum-study table. The rice-cooker was placed next to a stack of exercise books. Aside from a few plastic chairs, there is little furniture in this area. Not that there is much space for anything else. Since Mrs R was preoccupied with washing clothes and the only table was occupied by Mr R and me, this provided a good excuse for the two children to play in the corridors instead of doing their homework indoors. The only form of entertainment seems to be an old 14-inch colour TV set (perched on top of a chair) which delivered blurred images. No sofas. In the bedroom, a double bed occupied most of the space. This is where the family members sleep together. All the clothes are kept in the only foldable plastic 'wardrobe'. As there are no windows, a donated electronic fan eases the stuffiness in the room. Adjacent to the entire living space is the kitchen area where the family prepares its daily meals. Besides a small fridge, a kerosene and a portable electrical stove, there are some simple utensils and kitchenware.

After his dinner and a smoke, Mr R appeared more relaxed for me to interview him. The morning begins at 7:00 am for Mr R. Upon waking up, he takes a substantial meal of leftover rice and two eggs prepared by his wife. Then he cycles to work. The journey lasts about 15 minutes as his factory is located nearby. He is just on time for his 7:30 am–7:30 pm shift. I asked how he felt about his work, and he replied "like that lah" meaning he is fine with it. Work is alright, much of his time is spent patrolling and monitoring the CCTV. But with a 12-hour shift, and given the nature of his work, boredom inevitably sets in. Aside from coffee breaks with his colleagues, they read old newspapers or magazines to kill time ("relak"). The long shift work is so boring at times that a little commotion like the one he encountered this evening is the only thing that breaks the monotony of the day. Upon his return home, he has dinner and relaxes by watching television before turning in at 10:00 pm to prepare for the next day.

Coping strategies

When it comes to their monthly expenditure, Mr R explained that he sets aside $50 for himself and hands over the rest to his wife. When probed on how he spends his $50, Mr R appears rather vague and replies that most of it is spent on tobacco. (Since the price of cigarettes has risen, Mr R, being a heavy smoker, has resorted to rolling his own cigarettes with some paper and tobacco leaves.) Other than that, he neither handles any expenditure, nor is he aware of household finances as it is Mrs R who is in charge.

From my observations of Mr R's family on repeated visits, it amazes me the ways and means which Mrs R ingenuously employs to cut cost. Things which I take for granted become luxuries in a low-income household. Although there is a portable stove which uses piped gas, Mr R's family relies more regularly on the kerosene stove. When questioned why Mrs R prefers this arrangement, Mr R explained that it is much cheaper using kerosene. A tin container of kerosene could last them up to 1 month and at a cheaper cost than piped gas. Unlike the latter, which is liable to be cut off when bills are not paid, kerosene can be easily purchased in small quantities from nearby provision shops. Liquified petroleum gas (LPG) is an unpopular option simply because it cannot be purchased in small quantities and the one-time payment is considered too costly. The preference for kerosene stove in cooking explains the black fumes that stain the kitchen wall and the lingering smell. However, Mr R and his family appear to be accustomed to it.

Another method of cost cutting is to reduce the number of meals cooked everyday. Every morning, Mrs R cooks for all three meals: breakfast, lunch, and dinner. While serving her husband breakfast, the lunch portions are kept in a lunchbox for Mr R to take to work. The portions for dinner are refrigerated. During dinner time, these are heated and served with leftovers for tomorrow's breakfast. This helps them save on fuel and water. With the exception of Mr R, who eats three meals a day, the rest of the family subsist on two meals—breakfast and dinner. Most of the meals consist of instant noodles and maybe an egg because it is filling and economical. Rice is served occasionally and only at dinner time. This is eaten with a bit of fish and some vegetables bought cheaply from the market. In order to economize on her marketing, Mrs R buys only small fishes and leftover vegetables. Other seafood and meats like chicken, beef and mutton are considered luxuries in a low-income family.

Every fortnight, a volunteer social worker from the Community Development Council (CDC) checks on them. Besides house visits, Mr R receives some groceries like bread, milk, and rice. This helps to lighten his financial burden. In addition, the family refrains from eating out and buying new things. Mr R himself cycles to work, while his two children walk to school. Both of them have to make do with some hand-me-down clothing and donated toys. But some things must still be bought, e.g., assessment books.

Concerns

From our conversations about life in general, it is not difficult to surmise his main concern. On the one hand, he appeared laidback and contented, but on the other hand, he is anxious about present circumstances. Mr R explained that some years back, his wife was working as a hawker's assistant. This added to the family income. But due to her working hours, she had no time to look after the children. One day, a social worker came knocking at their door because his son, who was due for school, was not enrolled. This caused a rift between the couple because Mr R had assumed that his wife would take care of 'household' matters and was not sensitive to the fact that she was juggling work and family badly. The elder child was enrolled in a neighbourhood school, but he did not like school and was in the habit of playing truant. His teachers eventually came knocking and Mrs R reluctantly quit her job to look after the children.

When asked about his children's education, Mr R had to consult his wife. According to Mrs R, their elder child is rather playful. While she tries to make him finish his homework, she is not too sure if he has completed it. What she does know is that her son has not been doing very well in school. His teachers have frequently commented that although their son is rather bright, he has short attention span. His poor academic performance is exacerbated by his incompetent English. This affected his understanding of lessons in other subjects like Mathematics and Science. Their younger child, a daughter, is also facing the same problems in primary school. Much as Mrs R is worried about her children's education, she feels helpless as she is not able to coach them. Tuition is out of the question given the family's present circumstances. In fact, the children's school fees had been subsidised and some of their textbooks were donated to them. If not for these concessions, the parents would have difficulties supporting their children's studies.

It is also evident that Mr R is feeling the strain of being the sole breadwinner. During the interview, he frequently complained about not having enough money for the family and his children's education. His main grouse is the high cost of living ("…everything so expensive, need money") and increased expenses. Lately, there are some rumours circulating that the factory which occupies the building would be closing down. If the rumours prove to be true, then the building, which is owned by the factory, would also be closed down, putting him out of a job. Since times are bad, with an ongoing recession, he would face a lot of difficulties finding a new job, because he did not complete his primary education and is essentially unskilled. Despite his long shift, his current take home pay is about $700 per month; this is supplemented by an additional $200 from the CDC. Since the latter is given on a 3-monthly basis, it has to be renewed in a month's time. He pointed out that by then he would require more assistance but he may not be able to receive more benefits. If this happens, Mrs R would have to return to work to help support the family.

But in my last visit with Mr R, he appeared more contented than before. This probably has to do with the recent events which took place. Despite the rumours of closure, Mr R managed to keep his job as a security guard. Apparently, the factory in which he worked did not close down but merely retrenched some workers. In addition, the CDC renewed its monthly $200 benefits to his family. Meanwhile, Mrs R has found a weekend job as a banqueting worker. Clearly relieved at the way things had turned out, Mr R appeared more upbeat and talked about bringing his family to a meal at a fast-food restaurant the following week.

Case study 2

Living day by day: a working class man

Profile of Mr T

Age	: 41
Educational level	: Up to Secondary 2
Occupation	: Labourer at a wholesale vegetable market
Household Income	: About $1800 per month
Type of housing	: Three-room flat
Family	: Single, living alone

Everyday life

My first encounter with Mr T is at the wholesale vegetable market where he works. The large market bustles with activity as early as 5:00 am. Mr T works as a labourer for a distributor. His main task is to transport vegetables from buyers to sellers. Looking thin and wiry, his frame belies the amount of strength needed in this job.

According to Mr T, the vegetable wholesale market operates 24 hours. With advancement in transportation facilities, imported vegetables could arrive from China, Australia, Indonesia, and Malaysia much faster and in a fresher condition than before. Distributors work round the clock to receive their orders. Depending on the volume of their import, a distributor requires at least four labourers for a day's work, with each labourer on 12-hour shift 6 days a week. The working day for Mr T begins as early as 3:00 am when he is stationed at a particular vehicle lot waiting for a truckload of *kailan*. Subsequently, the Chinese cabbage, spinach, tomatoes, ladies fingers, and chillies arrive at between 15–30-minute intervals. Upon arrival, vegetables are collected from trucks and packed into crates; these are then carted away to the distributor. Since each labourer is familiar with the schedule of arrival and knows the exact amount of goods to carry, the process of transportation from truck to crate becomes as mechanically efficient as factory operation. Within 15 minutes, all goods are removed, packed and carted away.

At 5:00 am, another round of transactions takes place between the distributor and sellers. Mr T's task now is to transport the crates to the vegetable seller's lorries. It is obvious that his work revolves around the arrival of various imported vegetables. Although his working hours officially end at 3:00 pm, Mr T does not go home immediately after work. Instead, he tries to maximize his income by taking on some ad hoc duties. When one of the distributors' labourers was unable to turn up, he immediately approached Mr T to act as a replacement. Thus, his working period is sometimes lengthened by another 1 or 2 hours. But Mr T did not seem to mind; somehow he takes it in his stride. He feels that his job just requires some strength and very little thinking, as such, it is still manageable, whereas if he were a white-collar, he would *tao tia* ("have a headache") because of all that thinking and writing. The extra hours supplement his income considerably. Mr T revealed that he takes home about $2000 a month. He does not have any dependents other than his mother (he is single). All things considered, he is able to live comfortably with his income bracket.

Family background

Much of the interview was conducted in Hokkien, a Chinese dialect, simply because Mr T is most comfortable with it. This is hardly surprising given his educational background and environment. Bearing in mind that I am not conversant in dialect, he was considerate enough to speak in Mandarin, but he would lapse into his own dialect when he wanted to express nuances in certain phrases.

Mr T comes from a "complicated" background. His father, an odd job labourer, was an alcoholic. As far he could remember, his father was hardly around except to take money from his mother. During these rare occasions, he was physically abusive so much so that he and his sister would immediately hide under the bed when they heard his arrival. When Mr T was nine, his father left home, giving the family some respite. But he also left behind a pile of unpaid debts. The loansharks started hounding them to pay up. Fortunately, some relatives were sympathetic and Mr T's mother managed to get a loan to tide over the crisis. Subsequently, she worked very hard to support the family of three. As a child, Mr T was not particularly fond of school. He was resentful of many things and often quarreled with his mother. At school, he would get into serious fights with his classmates. Initially, the school was prepared to give the young Mr T another chance as he had been mathematically inclined. But he also joined secret societies and was actively involved in several gang fights. Shortly after, he was expelled from school.

Once out of school, he took on many "odd jobs". Although he did not mention it, it was implied that he was basically following his *tao* (the gang leader) around. Those were also the heady days of wine, women, and song (in the form of karaoke joints). Mr T also started dabbling with drugs like Ecstasy and Ketamine. His hedonistic pursuits came to an end when his gang mate died unexpectedly from brain seizure. His death was a shock to Mr T. What outraged Mr T was the way his gang members reacted to his gang mate's death. They were concerned only about whether the deceased left behind any clues that could implicate the gang in any way. After this, he sobered up, quit drugs, and kept his distance from the gang. With his friend's recommendation, he got himself his present job as a labourer and has been at it for almost 15 years. Since then, he has reconciled with his mother and married sister. Six years ago, when he finally qualified for flat application, he invited his mother to live with him.

When asked if he has any future plans (does he intend to get married and have a family?), Mr T replied that he is too old. Besides, he added, who would want to marry him? Local women are deemed as too stuck up, they would only consider someone who is higher in qualifications ("got Primary want Secondary, got Secondary want Poly...") or earn more in income. Since he feels that he meets neither condition, he considers himself non-eligible. Four years ago, his mother got someone to arrange a match for him with a distant relative from China. But the marriage plans fell awry when the potential bride demanded an exorbitant dowry. Recently, his mother had been asking him to consider Vietnamese brides but Mr T is not interested. He rationalizes that at his age, to get married and have children is to increase his burden. Thus, he has no such plans ("life is transient, you never know what will happen tomorrow"). Meanwhile he prefers to live day-to-day.

Recreation

Because Mr T works long and irregular hours, it is not surprising that his lifestyle has become somewhat unconventional. Early in the morning when most of us would be sleeping, he is already at work, while the afternoons have become his bedtime. As a result, the people he mixes with are almost exclusively his fellow labourers from the market. Besides his colleagues, he does not have other friends, even his only day off is mostly spent with them at coffeeshops, pubs, and karaoke joints.

During a hard day's work, there are also long hours' of breaks when he is free to wander around. According to his employer, Mr T can be found in the coffeeshop chatting with his colleagues. Another popular pastime is underground gambling, which is easily available in the market. This takes place in two forms: openly or furtively. Sometimes, the 'banker' sets up a make-shift stall and initiates a game of *puak kiao*, a simple betting game. In time, the few people gathering round become a small crowd of punters. Each game is necessarily fast paced because of possible raids from police. Another form of illegal gambling is in underground betting of 4D and Toto. Because of his gambling habits, Mr T does not save up as much as he should.

Although he is aware that his daily/weekly "investment" in this area is seldom repaid, Mr T remains defensive of his habits. To him, every bet is a chance to make some money. ("If you are lucky, one day you may *tiok tao pio* (win the first prize) but if you don't try, then you have no *xi wang* (hopes)"). Seen from another perspective, Mr T is rather realistic: his gambling represents a shot at the "Singapore Dream" without which he would not have any chance of owning the desired status symbols of cash, car, condominium apartment, credit cards, and club memberships.

Political views

Mr T is quite knowledgeable about current affairs, particularly local ones. His main source of information is the Chinese language evening tabloid that he enjoys reading daily. The tabloid also allows him to check on 4D and Toto results. He has many grouses: the GST hike, foreign workers, unemployment rate, among other things. He is critical of the government, yet not prepared to accept or imagine other political parties forming the government.

Aspirations

In my last interview with Mr T, I asked if he had any regrets in life. If, for example, he could turn back the clock to his teens again would he do anything different? He replied that if he had another chance at being young, he would start a business—any form of business ("maybe selling food, selling vegetables also can"). Then he would have been a *towkay* (boss) and need not work so hard for his living. There were no aspirations to be a white-collar professional or to be a respectable middle class man because he feels that in order to arrive at the latter, "you must be good at studying". White-collar jobs require too much thinking and it is too much of a hassle to observe dress codes, business etiquette, etc. As he is not interested in academic pursuits, Mr T feels that it is still better to be your own boss. But he concluded that it would be most useless regretting the past because "it is impossible to change it". Instead, one should just look ahead.

Case study 3

Decent living, mobile children: a working class parent

Profile of Mr W

Age	: 63
Educational level	: Primary level.
Occupation	: Taxi driver (day shift)
Household income	: About $2300 per month
Type of housing	: Four-room flat

Family : Household comprises wife (aged 56) and second son (aged 27); eldest daughter (aged 35) and first son (aged 34) are married and have their own households.

Family background and occupational history

The interview with Mr W, a taxi driver, did not start off very smoothly. Basically a taciturn man, he was not accustomed to being interviewed and would mostly stick to monosyllabic answers. From the little I picked out, however, I managed to piece his family background as such:

Mr W was born in 1940 to a large family. He is the eldest child. He had four sisters and two brothers. His father was a hawker and his mother, a washerwoman. He recalled living in an old shophouse in Bukit Ho Swee. During those days, the family shared a room with other tenants. Life was very hard in the post-war era, so Mr W gave up his studies to relieve his parents' burden.

Mr W's first job was as a rubber tapper. He recalled waking up early in the morning to collect the sap. During the heydays of rubber as an export commodity, an average taper earned 50 cents, a lucrative rate in an era when a meal cost only 5 cents. But the good days did not last very long, the price of rubber fell and almost overnight, it became a sunset industry, and Mr W had to look for another job. He then worked as a labourer for a rice merchant. The job involved transporting sacks of rice from ferry to warehouse and vice versa. For that he was paid 40 cents a day, a lower rate than his previous job, but, as he put it, "unemployment rate was very high, so workers were lucky if they had a job".

During this time, his family situation improved. His siblings had grown up and were able to support themselves. Having done his duty as an elder brother, Mr W felt he could now afford to settle down and start his own family. In 1967, he married his childhood sweetheart. But the years of hard labour took its toll on Mr W. Due to health reasons, he decided to try for a taxi licence.

He has been a taxi driver since 1973. He recalled that the period of greatest financial strain was when all three children were in school. In order to support his family, Mr W used to work very long shifts, allowing himself only 5–6 hours of sleep. At one point in time, he had to support both his daughter's and son's university studies. Both children had wanted to take up school loans, but his father was worried about putting them in debt. Neither of them qualified for scholarships, so both of them applied for bursaries to alleviate his financial burden. They worked during their school days as part-time tutors and during vacations to support themselves. When asked about his children, the pride in his answers was obvious. His eldest daughter and first son, who are both local graduates, are currently working in "respectable big companies". Both children are married and have moved out. His youngest son ("don't know what he is doing, something to do with drawing") still lives with him.

Lessons on life

When asked to "impart some lessons on life", Mr W said he believed in keeping a simple lifestyle. He wakes up at 6:30 am and starts work an hour later, knocking off at 6:00 pm. He has also kept his needs as simple as possible. Mr W does not drink or smoke (he was a heavy smoker in his younger days, but he quit 20 years ago when he had respiratory problems). Breakfast and dinner are taken at home. Lunch and coffee breaks are taken at the coffeeshop. He jokes that he still visits the same barber for 20 years, while his wife buys his shirts from the market ("cheap and lasting"). He has lived in his four-room flat for more than 30 years and he does not intend to move because he is too used to the neighbourhood. In his spare time, he watches some television, plays chess or catches up with his old friends.

When asked if he has any complaints about life in general, it took Mr W some time to come up with an answer. His only gripe is the "high cost of living in Singapore". Things are getting more expensive, he says. Take, for example, eating out. He tries to save by going to coffeeshops for meals. "Even foodcourt meals are not cheap. You pay $1 to $2 more for food and at least 50 cents more for drinks depending on where you go." He laments about the increase in GST and road tax. In addition, the economic downturn has affected his business. Previously he could pick up passengers from anywhere, but now he has to wait for some time at some popular spots for passengers to come. Moreover, there are more instances of passengers who haggle over the cab fare and some who got away without paying.

Now that his children have "grown up and are working", Mr W could easily afford to relax and take it easy. But retirement is far from his mind. Aside from the short family vacations, he says he is used to working and if he were to retire he would be very bored at home. In fact, he would like to continue working for as long as he could pass his annual road test.

Mr W's answer not only displays a strong work ethic but also a tenacity which derives from the harsh conditions of his childhood. Young people nowadays cannot take hardships, he says. They do not know how lucky they are to be living in an era of stability, free from wars and riots. He quotes the example of his young passengers who take a cab (even for short distances) when they could travel by bus or MRT. The same group of youngsters are also togged in branded clothes carrying fancy handphones but "the moment they open their mouth and talk, you know they don't come from rich families."

He pointed out that he himself did not have much education, but he managed to put his children through tertiary education. As long as one is willing to work hard one could easily make a decent living, although he agrees that success in life depends very much on paper qualifications. He believes that his children's qualifications and their career achievements are the best testimonies to this popular adage. His eldest daughter, who graduated in Accounting, is now an auditor, while his elder son is an engineer. Both children who are married have moved into executive maisonette and condominium, respectively. To Mr W, the only one who is faring less well but still making a good living is his younger son, a diploma holder currently working as a graphic artist. Mr W clearly belongs to a generation of Singaporeans who have braved through enough tumultuous times to appreciate the shade of economic prosperity.

Case study 4

Simple upgrading: a lower-middle class woman

Profile of Ms Z

Age	: 29
Educational level	: Polytechnic diploma, currently pursuing ACCA
Occupation	: Management Support Officer (MSO) Grade 3
Household Income	: About $2000 per month
Type of housing	: Five-room flat
Family	: Single, living with retired parents and younger sister (aged 21)

Although it was already 7:00 pm in the evening, the voice over the phone was one of chirpy congeniality. Hanging up, I waited for Ms Z to turn up for the first round of interview at a small café near her workplace.

Family background and education history

Ms Z is the eldest child in a family of four. Her father is a retired Malay teacher, while her mother is a housewife. Ms Z's younger sister, aged 21, is a graduate.

Ms Z recalls her childhood as a happy one. Her earliest memories were the days of playing *masak masak* (make-believe housewife involving toys like miniature household items) at home with her sister. In those days, the family lived in a three-room flat in Eunos, which is near her grandparents' flat in Marine Parade. As she sees it, her father is the disciplinarian in the family, whereas her mother is more forgiving and tolerant. Both parents were described as "strict but fair". For example, Ms Z and her sister were allowed to go out with friends after school provided they inform either parent in advance and return home before 9:00 pm. When the girls were older, at 18, the "curfew" extended to 11:00 pm. Ms Z does not find this rule particularly restrictive, since she sees it as a reflection of parental concern.

Ms Z entered primary one in a neighbourhood school near her house. Primary school was a culture shock to her. Being a sheltered child, she was awed by the large number of students in the school compound. She was also unused to English as the predominant language in school. This affected her progress in school, which resulted in her teacher asking to see her parents. This was considered a rather serious matter because parent–teacher meetings did not take place that frequently in the past. In most cases, teachers only requested to meet their students' parents if there were disciplinary or critical problems involved. Her teacher later arranged for Ms Z to attend remedial classes.

Ms Z did moderately well in her Primary School Leaving Examination (PSLE). Pleased with her progress, the family went on a short trip to Genting Highlands during her school holidays. She later attended a secondary school where she spent "the most fruitful period" of her school life. She was an active participant in sports and had many friends. Despite her active involvement in sports, which caused her parents much anxiety, she managed to "sail through" her 'O' level examinations.

Having passed her 'O' levels, Ms Z arrived at a decision point in her school career. Junior college and polytechnic education were the two most popular routes after 'O' levels. She qualified for both options. After much pondering, she decided to study accounting at the Singapore Polytechnic. She felt that it was a safer option and would be a shorter route to the job market. Her choice was also approved by her parents.

Career path

Upon graduation from the polytechnic, Ms Z joined the workforce as an officer at a local bank. She was posted to the credit department, a job which required her to "act like a loan shark". She found her job stressful and emotionally draining as she had to deal with bank clients in bad debts. On some occasions, Ms Z had had to do the dirty job of repossessing the private properties of debtors, including "chasing out the whole family—wife, two kids, and grandmother". In less than a year, she quit her post to join a public sector organization as a Management Support Officer (MSO).

In her second job, Ms Z was assigned to the Planning Office. Like her previous job, her new duties were totally unrelated to her accounting background. Work consisted of administrative duties like taking minutes, maintaining office systems and preparing submissions, tasks which Ms Z felt were "more manageable", in contrast to her previous job. But with her department expanding, Ms Z found herself being "shared" by four Senior Officers. She also had to take on additional clerical functions. This increased her workload tremendously, which resulted in her often having to remain in the office till 8:30 pm.

Fortunately, her long hours of hard work did not go unnoticed. Recognizing Ms Z's potential, her supervisor reduced her clerical duties and assigned her to more challenging projects. Ms Z's performance was so highly rated by her superiors that she won two promotions in her 7 years with the organization. However, she felt that, without higher qualifications, she would not be able to rise above MSO Grade 1. She did consider taking up part-time degree courses, but decided against doing so as she was under the impression that the organization does not recognize such qualifications. Moreover, she felt that her current workload does not allow her much time for part-time studies.

Future plans

As if to counter her frustrations at work, she frequently pampers herself by shopping, fine dining, going to movies, and spas. The latter are justified on the grounds that "I have worked very hard, so I am entitled to enjoy myself." Given her family situation, Ms Z could afford these occasional treats. She has no dependents as her parents are healthy and have their own savings, while her younger sister has recently secured a job right after graduation. But the situation will change when Ms Z gets married next year. She reveals that her fiancé is a clerical officer in another department, earning a lower salary. Considering their combined incomes, Ms Z felt that it would not be feasible to set up their own separate household; instead, the couple will live with her parents and use the savings from this arrangement, including other resources, to buy a lower-end car: "It would be nice to be chauffeured instead of squeezing with the rest of the horde in a long journey from Tampines to Buona Vista (where she works)…"

Case study 5

Challenges and opportunities: a middle class professional

Profile of Mr A

Age	: 39
Educational level	: University graduate
Occupation	: Senior manager in a design firm
Household income	: About $7000 per month
Type of housing	: Five-room flat
Family	: Wife (aged 35), daughter (aged 5) and son (aged 2)

Talking to Mr A was an interesting experience. During conversation, his hands would gesticulate frequently, and his voice alternating between animated excitement and cheerful optimism.

Social background of Mr A

Mr A was born in 1964 in India. As the only child and what was more, a son of a middle class family, Mr A's life was quite comfortable. His father was a businessman, while his mother was a housewife. But things changed when his father's business failed. The family sold their house and moved into a small apartment. They—and most of all, Mr A—found it difficult to adapt to their downgraded lifestyle. He soon realized that unless he secured a scholarship, his family resources would not be able to afford the exorbitant fees in top-rung universities.

Educational and occupational history

He eventually won a Colombo Plan Scholarship, which brought him to Singapore. After some initial struggles with homesickness and the new environment, Mr A proved himself to be quite adaptable. He even made it to the Dean's List, graduating with a first class honours in mechanical engineering in his final year.

Upon graduation, while most of his peers were knocking on the doors of multinational corporations (MNCs), Mr A decided to work for a local SME instead, a choice which surprised many of his classmates. In his view, working in an MNC is like working in any large organization with overly compartmentalized job scopes, which result in a person specializing in certain functions, but lacking a good understanding of how things are run. In contrast, working in an SME offers more challenges as its small size and structure forces a person to multi-task. This in turn exposes him to other aspects, such as business development, sales, marketing, and communications.

After his first job, Mr A moved to another local design firm. By then, he has not only accumulated vast experience, but also made a name for himself in the local scene. He was eventually headhunted to head the R&D department in the MNC which he now works for. Work is intense because he has to innovate and develop new concepts in order to clinch deals in the rather competitive business environment. What adds to the pressure is the challenge of meeting deadlines. Mr A says he enjoys his work very much as it is 'invigorating'. His long-term plan is to set up his own design firm as he believes there is definitely a niche for small design firms, given that "a lot of design work is being subcontracted nowadays".

Family life and recreation

Despite a hectic work schedule, Mr A makes it a point to spend weekends with his wife and two children. The family enjoys outings together at restaurants, picnics, trips to the zoo and the Science Centre. They visit India regularly, as well as made holiday trips to places in Australia, Canada, and Britain.

Mr A obtained his Singapore citizenship in 1997, the year he married his wife. The following year, he became a father when his daughter was born. After the birth of his son, Mrs A decided to quit her job as a dentist to look after their two children, a decision which is heartily approved by Mr A. As he sees it, "It is good that (Mrs A) would be able to look after them during their formative years, instead of relying on a maid." The desire to provide the best for their family also extends to the choice of school for their children. Plans for the children's education have also been made in advance. In order to qualify for the schools of their choice for primary school registration, the couple even moved residence from Eunos to Farrer Park.

When asked about his recreation, Mr A is unabashed in announcing that he enjoys window shopping for electronic goods. He makes it a point to visit Sim Lim Square at least once a week. Understandably, his hobby allows him to check out the newest gadgets in the market and provides new ideas for inspiration in his work. In this aspect, he admits that "he is very boring" as his hobby is "work-related". "Some people like to play golf, some like to look at cars, but I don't share those passions." As a testimony to his words, Mr A does not own a country club membership, and he travels to work in a second-hand Honda Civic.

Outlook on life

When asked if he has any concerns in life, Mr A shared that he remains upbeat despite the economic downturn which is preoccupying everyone's mind. As he put it: "I believe Singapore is a land of opportunity, particularly for those in IT industries. The basic infrastructure is already there. There will always be difficult challenges, but such challenges force everyone to innovate and improve..." This gung-ho can-do spirit also extends to his life philosophy: "If you want to make it, don't just sit there and whine. Instead, look around and try something different." He believes that success depends a lot on opportunities and networking. In his opinion, Singaporeans are not adept at the latter, and as a result have missed out on the former. He feels that Singaporeans have become too dependent on the government for solutions, and that they tend to be "overly sheltered and comfortable being led around."

Case study 6

Choices and dreams: an upper middle class life

Profile of Mr B

Age	: 42
Educational level	: University graduate
Occupation	: Senior business consultant
Household Income	: About $13 000 per month
Type of housing	: Four-room condo
Family	: Wife (aged 43) and son (aged 7)

It was quite difficult to fix an interview with Mr B. His schedule is so fully packed that what was supposed to be a two-session meeting was only made possible after taking up some of his lunch time. Looking at the man is to recognize the trappings of an established middle class person. Neatly togged in grey suit, there was a proverbial branded Mont Blanc fountain pen clipped to his breast pocket. On his left hand, he wears a Rolex watch. The accent he carried in his speech hints of his overseas education.

Everyday life

As a Senior Business Consultant, Mr B's job scope involves providing corporate solutions to his clients, be it brand imaging, sales improvement or public relations. The day at the office begins at 9:00 am sharp. The first hour is spent answering mails and making the required calls "to get things done". According to Mr B, the hours are spent in the following manner: attending meetings with clients to understand their needs, communicate on progress, and explain the approach; brainstorming sessions with his team of experts; and lastly, analysis of collected data. Unless there is corporate entertainment, the day ends at 9:00 pm. As some of his clients are foreign companies from the Asia Pacific region, his work requires him to fly (in Business Class) overseas once a month.

Family background and education history

Mr B came from a privileged family background. His father was a director in a shipping company, while his mother was a primary school teacher. He followed "the family tradition of studying at ACS (Anglo-Chinese School)". His fondest memories were those days spent climbing up the rambutan trees in the confines of his Katong house garden, catching spiders, playing *goh-lee* (marbles) in the *long kau* (large drains) with the kids next door.

Despite spending very little time on studying, he managed to top his class, something which he attributed more to luck as "school in those days was a breeze without streaming…" Things changed somewhat in secondary school, when Mr B became actively involved in swimming and debate. As both activities formed an integral part of school culture, there were many inter-class and inter-school competitions to prepare for, which took up a considerable amount of time. Besides these school activities, he also had to juggle violin lessons. He found himself having to practice good time management. To ensure that he could catch up with his classes, he had tuition lessons as a form of assurance. After his 'O' levels, Mr B attended ACJC (Anglo-Chinese Junior College). He continued to participate in swimming and debate, juggling both with his studies. Despite his heavy commitment to ECA (extra-curricular activities), his school work never suffered.

After the 'A' level results were released, Mr B, who was a Humanities Scholar, was in a quandary for a while. His good results qualified him for any programmes of his choice in the local universities. Coming from a humanities background, Mr B's interest leaned towards the Arts. His father agreed to send him overseas for a liberal arts education. At the overseas college, he found himself having to work harder to catch up in his grades. Lessons were also more challenging as the open-style of lecturing meant that questions could be asked at any time. It forced him to pay more attention and ask more questions.

Upon graduation, he decided to enrich his knowledge by taking an MBA "for a change". When I remarked about his good academic track record, Mr B brushed it aside, attributing it to his proper time management. Because he was either rehearsing or swimming, he made sure he paid attention during classes; something which he felt was very useful in revision. Another factor which he credited to his achievements was parental support. Mr B maintained that he was lucky in that while some of his classmates, who also had good academic results were "steered" towards the "normal stuff like Law and Medicine", his parents were supportive of his choice.

Family life and recreation

With a hectic work schedule at hand, there is little time for anything else. Whatever time he could spare is indeed "quality time". Moreover, his wife is equally busy in her career as a HR Manager. The couple, who met "through their work", are now proud parents to a 7-year-old son. When asked about his approach to raising his son, Mr B admitted that he is "like every other anxious parent". Unlike his parents who are more laidback, he has taken a more pro-active approach towards his only son. His wife has arranged for two tutors to coach their child in all subjects, and a piano teacher for his music lessons. He revealed that his son was initially not balloted for a place in his family's alma mater. With determination, Mr B appealed as a devoted alumni to the school board and "made a convincing plea". Fortunately, his effort paid off and his son enrolled in the school which Mr B considered "instrumental in cultivating his zest for life".

Mr B makes it a point to dine with his wife once a week, while Sundays are devoted to the rest of the family members. Eating out has become a popular way of spending their time together. His wife plans the annual family trip to far-off places. Last year, they went to Switzerland as "his mother liked the climate there and for (his son) to learn skiing". He joked that his recreation is also 'work-related'. He enjoys his round of golf at the Singapore Country Club where he meets up with friends and clients, thereby combining business and pleasure.

View on success

Having established his career and 'set up' a family, Mr B belongs to a privileged few who could be considered 'upper middle class'. As testimony to this comfortable lifestyle, his family owns a four-room condominium in a prime district, not just one but two cars (a Volkswagen Passat and Nissan Sunny), and expensive country club membership. When asked what he thought of his success, Mr B had an interesting opinion: "I feel that it (referring to financial accumulation) also depends on luck." Like many others, he is quick to point out the importance of paper qualifications, but he also attributes his accomplishment to his privileged background: "I think I am lucky in the sense that my parents have given me a good headstart." He pointed out that his parents provided him with his own space. They supported his decision to attend a liberal arts programme. The combination of liberal arts and business management degree is an invaluable asset in his future career. Most importantly, their liberal outlook gave him the opportunity to "pursue his own dreams". His father accepted his decision to work for another company, instead of joining the family business.

Mr B feels that success is not just about making money; it is also about being able to pursue one's dreams. For that reason, he is "seriously considering migration". Recently, Mr B was headhunted to join a US company, but he has turned it down due to emotional attachments to Singapore. However, there are mounting reasons to reconsider his options: better career options, child's education, displeasure with social, cultural, and political climate. The latter, he glosses over with a remark that "there are some things which he disagrees with" and refuses to answer more. Just as wealth affords greater choice, it also comes with greater expectations.

Appendix II

Opinion Research Questionnaire

Case Number: _____

Interviewer's Name: _____

Interviewer's Number: (_____) Team: _____

Date and time of visit: _____

No. of times visited: _____

Instruction to Interviewer:

Respondent must be a Singapore Citizen and who is in a position to answer the questionnaire.

Supervisor verification: _____

Introduction

Hello, my name is _____. I am an interviewer with… We would like to hear your opinions on some matters concerning life in Singapore. I will take about 20–30 minutes of your time. I would appreciate your cooperation and assistance. Please be assured that your answers will be kept strictly confidential.

Section A: Screening Questions/Demographics:

S1. Gender
1. Male
2. Female

S2. Ethnicity
1. Chinese
2. Malay
3. Indian
4. Other, *please specify* _____

S3. House Type
1. HDB 1-room
2. HDB 2-room
3. HDB 3-room
4. HDB 4-room
5. HDB 5-room
6. HDB Executive
7. Private Condominium/Apartment
8. Landed property
9. Other, *please specify* _____

S4. Which age group do you belong to? Age Group (as on your birthday this year)
00. Below 15 **(THANK AND TERMINATE)**

01. 15–19
02. 20–24
03. 25–29
04. 30–34
05. 35–39

06. 40–44
07. 45–49
08. 50–54
09. 55–59
10. 60–64

11. 65 or over **(THANK AND TERMINATE)**

S5. Are you a.... (Citizenship Status)?
1. Singapore Citizen

2. Singapore PR **(THANK AND TERMINATE)**
3. Employment Pass Holder **(THANK AND TERMINATE)**
4. Work Permit Holder **(THANK AND TERMINATE)**
5. Others **(THANK AND TERMINATE)**

Section B: Job History and Training

Instruction: **Definition of Work and Job** — For the purpose of this survey, when I ask you a question about **WORK or JOB**, I'd like you to think of it as being in paid employment, business, or self-employment **WITHOUT** being at the same time a **FULL-TIME** student, NSF personnel, homemaker, volunteer, and/or retiree.

Box A PREVIOUS JOB (Q1A)

1. Are you ...?
  1. a full-time student
  2. a NSFull-Time personnel
  3. a full-time homemaker
  4. a full-time volunteer
  5. currently not employed
  6. Working ☛ **GO TO BOX B**
2. Have you worked before? **(PLEASE NOTE DEFINITION OF WORK & JOB)**
  1. Yes
  2. No ☛ **GO TO Q1D**

3. What was your last **MAIN** job title? **(IF MORE THAN ONE, THEN MENTION ONLY WHAT THE RESPONDENT CONSIDERS TO BE HIS/HER MAIN JOB TITLE)**

   _____

4. What was your main job function? _____

5. What was the minimum qualification for this job? _____

   _____ **(GO TO BOX C)**

Box B CURRENT JOB (Q1B)

1. What is your **MAIN** job title? _____

2. What is your main job function? _____

3. What is the minimum qualification for this job? _____

4. Is your job (Read answer from below) _____?
   1. Permanent   2. Contractual   3. Temporary

   If in BUSINESS or SELF-EMPLOYMENT,

5. How would you rate the prospects of your business over the next 5 years? *(Single Answer)*
   1. Very Poor
   2. Poor
   3. Average
   4. Good
   5. Very Good
   6. NA **(DON'T READ)** ☞ **GO TO BOX C**

   If in PAID EMPLOYMENT,

6. How would you rate your prospects for advancement in your **MAIN** job over the next 5 years? *(Single Answer)*
   1. Very Poor
   2. Poor
   3. Average
   4. Good

5. Very Good
6. NA **(DON'T READ)**

7. How would you rate your prospects for skills upgrading/professional development in your **MAIN** job over the next 5 years? *(Single Answer)*
   1. Very Good
   2. Good
   3. Average
   4. Poor
   5. Very Poor
   6. NA **(DON'T READ)**

Box C FIRST JOB (Q1C)
1. Is the job described in Box A or Box B above your first **MAIN** job? **(PLEASE NOTE DEFINITION OF WORK & JOB)**   1. Yes ☞ **GO TO Q1D**   2. No   2. What was your first **MAIN** job title? _____   3. What was your main job function? _____   4. What was the minimum qualification for your this job? _____

1D. Generally speaking, what was/is the financial situation of your family when you were growing up, that is, when you were/are **about** 15 years old? Would you say your family was poor, or average, better than average, or well-off? *(Single Answer)*
   1. Poor   2. Average
   3. Better than average   4. Well-off

1E. Could you tell me what was the **HIGHEST** level of education your father had attained? (e.g., If passed Sec 1, then Option 4 is applicable.) *(Single Answer)*
   1. None
   2. Primary level
   3. PSLE/Certificate in Best 4
   4. Secondary level

5. N/O level
6. Vocational institute/National Trade Certificate level (NTC 3)
7. ITE/National Trade Certificate level (NTC 1 or 2)
8. Pre-U/JC/A-level
9. Polytechnic Diploma level
10. University level (undergraduate, postgraduate degree)
11. Professional qualifications (e.g. ACCA),

please specify _____.

1F. IF WORKING, what is your father's **MAIN** job? **(IF not working, then mention his previous job, if any).**

Job title: _____

Main job function: _____

1G. Could you tell me what was the **HIGHEST** level of education your mother had attained? *(Single Answer)*
1. None
2. Primary level
3. PSLE/Certificate in Best 4
4. Secondary level
5. N/O level
6. Vocational institute/National Trade Certificate level (NTC 3)
7. ITE/National Trade Certificate level (NTC 1 or 2)
8. Pre-U/JC/A-level
9. Polytechnic Diploma level
10. University level (undergraduate, postgraduate degree)
11. Professional qualifications (e.g. ACCA), *please specify*

_____.

1H. What is the **HIGHEST** level of education you have attained? *(Single Answer)*
1. None ☛ **GO TO Q1L**
2. Primary level
3. PSLE/Certificate in Best 4
4. Secondary level
5. N/O level

6. Vocational institute/National Trade Certificate level (NTC 3)
7. ITE/National Trade Certificate level (NTC 1 or 2)
8. Pre-U/JC/A-level
9. Polytechnic Diploma level
10. University level (undergraduate, postgraduate degree)
11. Professional qualifications (e.g. ACCA), *please specify*
_____.

1J. What was your first language when you were in primary school? *(Single Answer)*

1K. What about secondary school? *(Single Answer)*

	1J. Primary school	1K. Secondary school
No secondary education	1	1
English only as first language	2	2
Chinese only as first language	3	3
Malay only as first language	4	4
Tamil as first language	5	5
Both English and Chinese as first languages	6	6
Both English and Malay as first languages	7	7
Both English and Tamil as first languages	8	8
Others, please specify	9	9

_____

1L. Are you currently enrolled in any vocational/academic/professional courses (refer to courses that have a bearing on current/future job/career options/opportunities)?
1. Yes ☛ **GO TO Q1N**
2. No

1M. Are you planning to enroll in any vocational/academic/professional courses over the next 5 years (refer to courses that have a bearing on current/future job/career options/opportunities)?
1. Yes
2. No ☛ **GO TO Q1P**

1N. If **YES**, which level of courses are you enrolled in/planning to enroll in?
   1. Primary level
   2. PSLE/Certificate in Best 4
   3. Secondary level
   4. N/O level
   5. Vocational institute/National Trade Certificate level (NTC 3)
   6. ITE/National Trade Certificate level (NTC 1 or 2)
   7. Pre-U/JC level
   8. Polytechnic Diploma level
   9. University level (undergraduate, postgraduate degree)
   10. Professional qualifications (e.g. ACCA), *please specify* _____.

1P. Have you ever considered going into business/self-employment?
   1. Yes
   2. Already in business/self-employment ☞ **GO TO 1R**
   3. No ☞ **GO TO 1R**

1Q. If YES, what are the chances that you would go into business/self-employment over the next 5 years? *(Single Answer)*
   1. very low
   2. low
   3. neither low nor high
   4. high
   5. very high

1R. How satisfied are you with your life? *(Single Answer)*
   1. Very satisfied
   2. Satisfied
   3. Not Satisfied
   4. Not satisfied at all.

Section C: Financial Situation

2A. How would you describe your present financial situation? *(Single Answer)*
   1. Poor
   2. Average

118 Appendix II

      3. Better than Average
      4. Well-off

2B. What do you think your financial situation would be like over the next 5 years?
      1. Worse than now
      2. About the same as now
      3. Better than now

2C. How many persons are there in your household (including the respondent)?_____
(Definition: If not a one-person household, the term "household" refers to two or more persons living in the same house and sharing common food or other arrangements for essential living, but excluding live-in maids.)

2D. Looking back at your **household** incomes and expenditures for the last three months, would you say that your household incomes were more than, less than, or equal to your household expenditures? *(Single Answer)*
      1. More than
      2. Equal to
      3. Less than

2E. Is your household receiving financial support from outside the household? *(Read Out Definition of Household at Q2c)*
      1. No ☞ **GO TO Q2G**
      2. Yes

2F. From whom does your household receive financial support? *(Single Answer)*
      1. relatives
      2. friends
      3. charitable/voluntary/religious organizations
      4. relatives and friends
      5. relatives/friends and charitable/voluntary/religious organizations

2G. Do you or any member of your household (abbreviation: HHM) requires the services of one or more of the following social agencies or programmes? *(If Yes, Please Proceed to Columns 2,3, And 4)*

		1. Do you or any HHM require this service?		IF YES, REQUIRE SERVICES					
Social Agencies or programmes				2. Have you or any HHM made use of this service during the past year?		3. Do you or any HHM (find it/ think it is) convenient to use this service?		4. Do you or any HHM (find it/ think it is) affordable, i.e., within your means?	
		Yes	No	Yes	No	Yes	No	Yes	No
1.	Crisis shelters	1	2	1	2	1	2	1	2
2.	Home shelters for the aged	1	2	1	2	1	2	1	2
3.	Homes for the disabled	1	2	1	2	1	2	1	2
4.	Vocational assessment programme	1	2	1	2	1	2	1	2
5.	Day activity centers for the disabled	1	2	1	2	1	2	1	2
6.	Counseling centers (for domestic violence and abuse)	1	2	1	2	1	2	1	2
7.	Family service centers	1	2	1	2	1	2	1	2
8.	Student care centers	1	2	1	2	1	2	1	2
9.	Child care centers	1	2	1	2	1	2	1	2
10.	Seniors activity centers	1	2	1	2	1	2	1	2
11.	Social day centers for the aged	1	2	1	2	1	2	1	2
12.	Befriender service (volunteer programme for the lonely elderly)	1	2	1	2	1	2	1	2

Section D: Orientations

3A. Rank the importance of the following for achieving success in Singapore? **(1 = most important, 5 = least important)**

Attributes	Rank
1. Ability	
2. Education	
3. Hard work	
4. Knowing the right people	
5. Luck	

3B. How much influence do you think you as a citizen **should have** on national issues? *(Single Answer)*
1. A great deal
2. Some Influence
3. Little or no influence.

3C. How much influence do you think **citizens like yourself** have on national issues? *(Single Answer)*
1. A great deal
2. Some Influence
3. Little or no influence

3D. Do you think most people would try to take advantage of you if they got the chance, or would they try to be fair?
1. Take advantage
2. Try to be fair

3E. Please tell me whether you **Strongly Agree, Agree, Disagree, or Strongly Disagree** with the following statements **(If not applicable, please circle NA):**

Opinion Research Questionnaire

ATTRIBUTES	SA	A	N	D	SD	NA
1. Everyone in Singapore has a good chance to achieve a high standard of living.	1	2	3	4	5	99
2. The government should give financial assistance to the poor.	1	2	3	4	5	99
3. People who are more successful have a responsibility to help the less successful ones.	1	2	3	4	5	99
4. All things considered, Singapore has more good points than bad points.	1	2	3	4	5	99
5. I am proud to be a Singaporean.	1	2	3	4	5	99
6. Successful people in Singapore tend to look down on the less successful ones.	1	2	3	4	5	99
7. I don't have much in common with Singaporeans of other races.	1	2	3	4	5	99
8. It is not always wise to plan too far ahead because many things turn out to be a matter of good or bad fortune anyway.	1	2	3	4	5	99
9. We can try our best, but finally, it is the powerful people who decide whether we succeed or not.	1	2	3	4	5	99
10. Working people in Singapore should join unions.	1	2	3	4	5	99
11. Singapore unions ensure that their members are treated fairly.	1	2	3	4	5	99
12. I am quite comfortable with using the computer.	1	2	3	4	5	99
13. My lack of ability in using the computer will hinder my finding a job or hinder my career advancement.	1	2	3	4	5	99

ATTRIBUTES	SA	A	N	D	SD	NA
14. I find it difficult to provide financial support to my parents.	1	2	3	4	5	99
15. I find difficult to provide financial support to my spouse and children.	1	2	3	4	5	99
16. I find it difficult to provide financial support to my siblings.	1	2	3	4	5	99
17. Singapore is not a good place to make a living.	1	2	3	4	5	99
18. Singapore is a good place to raise one's children.	1	2	3	4	5	99
19. I am confident that my financial situation will improve in the next 5 years.	1	2	3	4	5	99
20. I believe my prospect for career advancement in the next 5 years is good.	1	2	3	4	5	99
21. I have close friends who are of a different race.	1	2	3	4	5	99
22. I do not have close friends who are from lower income groups.	1	2	3	4	5	99
23. I have close friends who are from higher income groups.	1	2	3	4	5	99
24. I believe the generation after mine will have a brighter future than my generation.	1	2	3	4	5	99
25. I support the idea of having people of different races living in the same housing estate.	1	2	3	4	5	99

Section E: Self-identification

4A. Suppose we classify Singaporeans into the following six classes. In which class would you put yourself? (If unable to decide, then choose the class that comes closest to the one you feel you belong in.) *(Single Answer)*
   1. Upper class
   2. Upper middle class
   3. Middle middle class
   4. Lower middle class
   5. Upper lower class
   6. Lower lower class

4B. Suppose we **instead** classify Singaporeans into the following 4 classes. In which class would you put yourself? (If unable to decide, then choose the class that comes closest to the one you feel you belong in.) *(Single Answer)*
   1. Upper Class
   2. Middle Class
   3. Working Class
   4. Lower Class

Section F: Other demographics

5A. What is your marital status?
   1. Single, never married ☛ **GO TO Q5E**
   2. Married
   3. Divorced/Separated
   4. Widowed

5B. **IF MARRIED/EVER MARRIED**, How many children do you have?
   1. None
   2. One
   3. Two
   4. Three
   5. More than Three

5C. Could you tell me what is the **HIGHEST** level of education your spouse/ex-spouse/late spouse had attained?
   1. None
   2. Primary level
   3. PSLE/Certificate in Best 4
   4. Secondary level
   5. N/O level
   6. Vocational institute/National Trade Certificate level (NTC 3)
   7. ITE/National Trade Certificate level (NTC 1 or 2)
   8. Pre-U/JC/A-level
   9. Polytechnic Diploma level
   10. University level (undergraduate, postgraduate degree)
   11. Professional qualifications (e.g. ACCA), please specify
   _____

5D. IF your spouse/ex-spouse/late spouse is/was WORKING, what is/was his/her **MAIN** job (IF not working, then mention his/her previous job, if any.)

   Job title: _____

   Main job function: _____

5E. What is your religion?
   1. Buddhism
   2. Taoism
   3. Traditional Chinese Religion (Shenism)
   4. Islam
   5. Hinduism
   6. Christianity – Charismatic, Pentecostal, Methodist, Presbyterian, or other non-Catholic Christian denomination or non-denominational group),
   7. Christianity – Catholicism
   8. Other Religion, please specify _____
   9. No Religion

5F. What is your gross monthly **Personal** income?
   1. Below $1000
   2. $1000–1999

3. $2000–2999
4. $3000–3999
5. $4000–4999
6. $5000–5999
7. $6000–6999
8. $7000–7999
9. $8000–8999
10. $9000–9999
11. $10,000 and above

5G. What is your gross monthly **household** income?
1. Below $1000
2. $1000–1999
3. $2000–2999
4. $3000–3999
5. $4000–4999
6. $5000–5999
7. $6000–6999
8. $7000–7999
9. $8000–8999
10. $9000–9999
11. $10,000 and above

Interviewer's Remarks/Comments:

_____

_____

_____

_____

_____

Particulars of Respondent

Address: _____

Tel no : Home _____ Office _____

        : H/p _____ Pager _____

Name of respondent: _____

E-mail: _____

Acknowledgement

I, _____ hereby received a token of $5.00 voucher from the above interviewer.

Serial no: _____

Respondent signature: _____

Date: _____

Thank you very much for your time today. We appreciate hearing your opinions.

Bibliography

Barber, Bernard, 1957. *Social Stratification: A Comparative Analysis of Structure and Process.* New York: Harcourt, Brace, & Co.
Bottomore, Tom, 1965. *Classes in Modern Society.* London: Allen and Unwin.
Brown, Roger, 1965. *Social Psychology.* New York: Free Press.
Byrne, David, 1999. *Social Exclusion.* Buckingham: Open University Press.
Chen, Peter S. J., 1975. "Growth and Income Distribution in Singapore". Paper presented at the International Symposium on *Criteria and Measurements of Income Distribution and Redistribution in Developing Countries,* April 28–May 1, 1975.
Chiew, Seen Kong, 1991. "Social Mobility in Singapore", in Quah, Stella, Chiew Seen Kong, Ko Yiu Chung, and Sharon Lee Meng Chee, eds., *Social Class in Singapore.* Singapore: Centre for Advanced Studies/Times Academic Press.
Chua, Beng Huat and Tan Joo Ean, 1999. "Singapore: Where the Middle Class Sets the Standard", in Pinches, Michael, ed., *Culture and Privilege in Capitalist Asia.* London/New York: Routledge.
Department of Statistics, Singapore, 2001. *Census 2000 Figures* (unpublished). Singapore: Department of Statistics.
Edgell, Stephen, 1993. *Class.* London: Routledge.
Evans, Geoffrey, 1994. "Class Conflict and Inequality", in *International Social Attitudes: The 10th BSA Report.* Aldershot, England: BSA.
Housing and Development Board, 2000. *Profile of Residents Living in HDB Flats.* Singapore: Research and Planning Department, HDB.

Jones, David M. and David Brown, 1994. "Singapore and the Myth of the Liberalizing Middle Class". *The Pacific Review*, 7(1): 79–87.

Mak, Lau Fong, 1993. "The Rise of the Singapore Middle Class: An Analytical Framework", in Hsiao Michael H. H. ed., *Discovery of the Middle Classes in East Asia*. Taipei: Academia Sinica.

Mak, Lau Fong, 1997. "Between Materialism and Post-Materialism: The Addicted Middle Class in Singapore". PROSEA Occasional Paper No. 8. Taipei: Academia Sinica.

Marshall, Gordon, 1997. *Repositioning Class: Social Inequality in Industrial Societies*. London: Sage.

Quah, Stella; Chiew, Seen Kong; Ko, Yiu Chung; and Lee Sharon, eds. 1991. *Social Class in Singapore*. Singapore: Centre for Advanced Studies/Times Academic Press.

Rempel, Michael and Terry Nichols Clark, 1997. "Post-Industrial Politics: A Framework for Interpreting Citizen Politics Since the 1960s" in Terry, Nichols Clark and Rempel Michael, eds., *Citizen Politics in Post-Industrial Societies*. Boulder: Westview Press.

Rodan, Garry, 1993. *Singapore Changes Guard: Social, Political and Economic Directions in the 1990s*. New York: St. Martin's Press.

Rodan, Garry, 1996. "Class Transformations and Political Tensions in Singapore's Development", in Robison, Richard, and Goodman, David S. G. eds., *The New Rich in Asia: Mobile phones, McDonalds, and Middle Class Revolution*. London: Routledge.

Tan, Ern Ser, 2000. "Workplace Power in Singapore: A Paradox? Evidence from a 1998 National Survey". *Labour and Management in Development Journal*, 1(8): 2–13.

Yao, Souchou, 1996. "Consumption and Social Aspirations of the Middle Class in Singapore". *Southeast Asian Affairs 1996*. Singapore: Institute of Southeast Asian Studies.

Zweig, Michael, 2000. *The Working Class Majority: America's Best Kept Secret*. Ithaca: Cornell University Press.

Index

ability 2, 12, 21–25, 52, 61–62, 71, 84, 120–121
age 16–17, 20, 22–29, 31–33, 37–42, 44–48, 50–52, 56, 59–61, 63, 67, 83–87, 92, 95–96, 100, 103, 105, 111

career advancement 10, 12, 61–62, 121–122
career strategies 47, 51
Census 2000 4, 10–13, 17
class 1, 7, 9, 20, 47, 59, 68, 83, 92
class and ethnic relations 1, 7
class map 9–10, 15
class structure
  four-category class structure 10, 13–16
  six-category class structure 13–15
classless society 2, 5
cluster analysis 10
cross-class ties 36
cross-ethnic ties 36–37, 39, 84, 86

democracy 32, 35
digital divide 1, 59, 63, 85–86
downward mobility 5, 55–56

equality of opportunity 2, 6, 21
ethnicity 8, 16–24, 26–28, 30–34, 38–51, 53, 55, 57, 59–61, 64, 68, 83–86, 111

Goldthorpe 9, 11

housing type 12–13, 15, 67

income security 4
intermediate class 10–12, 28, 54, 68, 85

job security 10, 12

life satisfaction 42–44, 77–78, 86
life-chances 2–3, 6
lower class 13–14, 17, 21, 23, 25, 34, 37, 49, 55–56, 58–59, 64, 68, 71, 74, 84–85, 123
luck 21–23, 25, 71, 84, 106, 108, 120

meritocracy 6, 21
middle class 1–5, 9, 11–15, 17, 19, 21, 33–36, 42, 46, 55–56, 58, 83–84, 96, 103, 106, 123
middle-class society 1–5, 11

one-to-three-roomers 66, 85
one-to-two-roomers 66–68, 71, 73–74, 76–79, 81–82, 85
opportunity 1–2, 7, 24–25, 37, 52, 71, 84, 86, 105, 109

participation opportunity 32–36, 73, 84, 86
participation propensity 32–34, 36, 73, 84, 86
political alienation 32–36, 73–74, 84, 86
political participation 1, 7, 32, 73, 84, 86
poor 3, 5, 14, 25–26, 48–51, 56–58, 70–72, 75–76, 91, 113–114, 117, 121

recession 4, 10–12, 20, 39, 42, 91

sandwich generation 1, 59, 63, 78, 80, 85–86
service class 10–12, 17, 54–55, 68
skills upgrading 5, 47, 49–52, 76–77, 85–86, 114
social agencies 7, 78–82, 119

social connection 21–23, 25, 84
social mobility 1–3, 16, 42, 47, 53–56, 84, 86
social orientations 1, 5, 7, 10–11, 20, 67, 71, 73, 83, 85
social services
 affordability 80–81
 convenience 80
stratification 1, 5–6, 9, 13, 17, 19
subjective class structure 13
success factors 21–23, 71, 73, 83–85

unionism 1, 7, 28, 31–32, 84
upper class 13–14, 23, 25, 28, 34, 44, 56, 58, 123

welfare policy 12
welfarism 1, 6–7, 25, 27, 84
working class 3–5, 9–12, 14–15, 21–22, 25, 28, 43, 52, 54–56, 58–59, 61, 64, 68, 74, 84–85, 92, 96, 123
Wright 9